Once Upon an Innovation

A **Business Storytelling Guidebook**
for Creative Problem Solving

JEAN STORLIE AND **MIMI SHERLOCK**

BEAVER'S POND
PRESS

Logic will get you from A to B.
Imagination will take you everywhere.

—ALBERT EINSTEIN

FourSight visual model, which appears in the Introduction and is referenced throughout the book, was developed by Nielsen and Thurber in 2011, based on the work of Puccio and Miller, 2003. It was first published in *Creativity Unbound: An Introduction to Creative Process*, 2011. Used with permission from FourSight and Creative Education Foundation.

The story "The Cookie Thief" by Valerie Cox, which appears in chapter 3, is from *A 3rd Serving of Chicken Soup for the Soul* by Jack Canfield and Mark Victor Hansen © 2012 by Chicken Soup for the Soul Publishing, LLC. Published by Backlist, LLC, a unit of Chicken Soup for the Soul Publishing, LLC. Chicken Soup for the Soul is a registered trademark of Chicken Soup for the Soul Publishing, LLC. Reprinted by permission. All rights reserved.

Edited by Wendy Weckwerth
Illustrated by Abigail Harkness
Production editor: Hanna Kjeldbjerg

ISBN 13: 978-1-59298-601-9
Library of Congress Catalog Number: 2019906464
Printed in the United States of America
First Printing: 2020
24 23 22 21 20   5 4 3 2 1

Book design and artistic direction by Dan Pitts. Typesetting by Jean Storlie.
Interior is set in Perpetua.

BEAVER'S POND
PRESS

939 Seventh Street West
Saint Paul, MN 55102
(952) 829-8818
www.BeaversPondPress.com

To order, visit www.ItascaBooks.com
or call (800) 901-3480 ext. 118. Reseller discounts available.
Contact Jean Storlie at www.storlietelling.com for speaking engagements, book club discussions, storytelling training, innovation and problem-solving projects, and interviews.

Contents

Foreword

As someone who has spent a career practicing and learning the many paths forward to successful innovation and advancing change, I have read countless books and articles on the topic. Among all these titles, I found *Once Upon an Innovation* to be a particularly valuable guidebook with insights and strategies about how to leverage the power of storytelling to grab attention, inspire new thinking, and motivate action.

There is much to like about *Once Upon an Innovation*, but I'll just highlight three things and urge you to find more in your own experience with this terrific book. First, as a book about storytelling, I really appreciate that real stories are incorporated to begin each chapter. Not only do they highlight how inspiring stories can stimulate one's imagination, they are also useful introductions in foreshadowing the content of the chapter. Secondly, for me this book feels much more like a "how-to" book than an academic textbook, balancing theories with useful examples of how to apply the learning. Finally, I've repeatedly experienced that uncovering a creative insight is only half the battle in achieving innovation—implementing that new idea through the various hazards and challenges (that are often present within any organization) is equally critical. Jean and Mimi's writing is very pragmatic in offering ways to navigate and align support within an organization through the utilization of stories in a way that I haven't seen before in other innovation books.

I think many will agree that achieving successful innovation can be a tough challenge, requiring plenty of inspiration, lessons learned from experience, and the thoughtful use of the right tools. I found that *Once Upon an Innovation* generously offers all three of these key elements.

In addition to marketers, insight professionals, engineers/scientists, and product developers, others can apply the lessons and approaches highlighted in *Once Upon an Innovation*. I can see plant production managers, government leaders, schoolteachers, and social entrepreneurs benefiting from this book. Virtually anyone focused on advancing change or driving meaningful improvements can learn from this content.

I hope that this book helps your efforts in supporting creativity and leading change wherever you are.

—Peter Erickson
Retired Executive Vice President
Innovation, Technology, and Quality
General Mills

Introduction

Once Upon . . .

We rarely get to choose where unexpected inspiration hits. Turns out, sometimes it strikes in a cafeteria.

On a meal break during the 2014 Creative Problem Solving Institute (CPSI) conference, we (Jean and Mimi) sat in a secluded booth nestled between the dessert selection and tray return. We'd just shared a lightbulb moment: as a duo we're uniquely suited to address the intersection where storytelling meets creative problem solving. With cafeteria trays clattering in the background, we dreamed of ways to merge our talents. Within twenty minutes we'd hatched a plethora of schemes and possibilities for how we might collaborate. When we parted ways, our brains swirled with ideas.

Soon after, we bid on a couple of consulting proposals together. During those collaborations, we experienced a mind meld that was intensely creative and productive. We learned that our skills, talents, and approaches are complementary and synergistic. And working together was seamless—it felt almost magical. Mimi would produce an initial brain dump of ideas and possibilities. Jean would build, refine, and pull all the pieces together into a clear and coherent communication. It felt easy and energizing. But after that professional nirvana our lives went in slightly different directions.

After nine successful years with Sherlock Creative Thinking, Mimi was finding the life of an independent consultant a bit lonely. As an extrovert, she missed the energy of working as part of a team. She decided to return to the corporate world to take a dream job.

Coming off a corporate layoff and a "sabbatical" year of severance, Jean was gaining traction with her new consultancy, Storlietelling LLC. The proposals she developed with Mimi fired her passion to explore how storytelling could be merged with innovation and creative problem solving facilitation. The experience helped her cement a new focus. She started to develop a book concept to explore this new direction. Just as Mimi reentered corporate life, Jean began to research and conceptualize what became *Once Upon an Innovation*.

Then in 2017 we revisited our collaboration to co-create a training workshop, "Storytelling in Innovation," for that year's CPSI conference. By that time Jean had started writing her book, and the workshop became a valuable test lab. In late 2018 Mimi brought fresh energy to the book project just when Jean was hitting a wall in her writing marathon. Mimi provided thought leadership, ideas, resources, and support. We began another intense sprint of collaboration that culminated in the book you're reading now.

We bring to this book inspiration and expertise from the creative problem solving and business storytelling movements, along with our own scientific backgrounds and corporate experience. Many innovation and creativity books point to the value of stories, but they fall short of showing how to develop and use stories. Some business storytelling books gesture toward the use of stories in critical innovation skills—such as visioning, collaborating, leading change, and empowering others—but don't link their methods to the innovation process.

This book explores the space between business storytelling, creative collaboration, and innovation to examine how story-based tools and techniques can enable innovation and creative problem solving from both theoretical and practical perspectives. We show how strategically relevant stories can rally stakeholders and a team around a vision and how story techniques bring empathy and human emotions into the conceptual process to generate rich and meaningful ideas. We guide you in the use of stories to bring formative ideas and refined concepts to life for testing and prototyping. We hope this book helps you become a skilled storyteller who persuades and inspires others.

Leveraging *Once Upon an Innovation*

This book is a resource for a wide range of professionals participating in innovation—marketers, insights professionals, engineers, scientists, product developers, and those who lead and facilitate innovation and creative problem solving processes.

Marketers and insights professionals can benefit from learning methods of storytelling to turn insights into stories and energize their teams. Technical experts can benefit from learning the art and science of stories to spark their imagination and communicate with empathy and vision. Business leaders and human resources professionals inside companies can use the resources to accelerate innovation and manage the organizational changes innovation often brings. Consultants and facilitators who support innovation processes will find inspiration and practical tools to help them design and facilitate emotionally engaging, high-impact events and processes.

This book has broad applications beyond business and industry. Leaders from public, private, and nonprofit organizations can use the tools and techniques in this book to lead change and inspire others.

Defining *Story*

Storytelling has become a buzzword of the business world and in our broader culture. As people toss around the term, they don't always mean the same thing. Some people think of a *story* as fiction. Others view any real-life event told in the first person as a *story*. Journalists call news articles *stories*. Quotes, testimonials, anecdotes, case studies, and scenarios are sometimes called *stories*. These communications may or may not contain the three elements that must be present to tell a character-driven story: character, struggle, and change.

We base our understanding of *story* on neuroscientific evidence about how a narrative affects brain chemistry and imparts empathy. Our perspective is also informed by how our forerunners in the business storytelling movement define a story. We believe a story shares an event or series of events by describing the people, place, and action, along with emotional context. Here's the definition of story at the foundation of this book:

An episode—real or imagined—that depicts a character struggling against an obstacle that may or may not be overcome. The struggle leads to a new understanding or truth, and an emotional transformation.

Emotional transformation—also called *catharsis*—differentiates a story from an amusing anecdote. A vivid portrayal of how a character changes as a result of a struggle will connect with people at a visceral level. Catharsis is the most vital element of a story.

History

It's impossible to speak about storytelling as an innovation tool without discussing the origin of two practices. Our fusion of business storytelling and creative problem solving parallels how these practice areas emerged. Both hinged on collaboration and were fueled by synergistic unions. The CPSI story is a fusion of advertising and academic talents in a collaboration that spawned a global community. The business storytelling movement merged the folksy and entertaining world of storytelling with the serious corporate world.

CPSI is the oldest and longest-running creativity conference in the world. It was the brainchild of Alex Osborn, the co-founder of the advertising firm BBDO, and Sid Parnes, a professor at Buffalo State College (located in Buffalo, New York) and the co-founder of the International Center for Studies in Creativity. Osborn is credited with being the inventor of brainstorming and the founder of the Creative Education Foundation (CEF), the nonprofit organization that presents CPSI.

Osborn and Parnes created a six-step creative problem solving process (known as Osborn-Parnes CPS), which inspires practitioners who apply creative problem solving to business, education, art, science, and a plethora of other challenges.

In 2011, CEF adopted a simplified version of Osborn-Parnes CPS that was developed and validated by Gerard Puccio, PhD, chair of the Creative Studies Department at Buffalo State

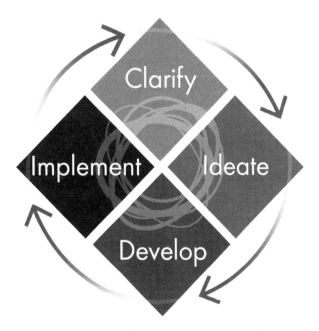

FourSight visual model. Used with permission from FourSight and Creative Education Foundation.

College, and published by FourSight®. The streamlined, iterative process of diverging and converging to define and tackle challenges involves four phases:

Clarify—Define the right problem to solve.

Ideate—Generate a range of possible solutions and select ideas with high potential.

Develop—Refine, strengthen, and polish high-potential ideas.

Implement—Prepare to turn ideas into actionable products and services.

When storyteller Doug Lipman met corporate trainer Annette Simmons in the mid-1990s at a storytelling festival, storytelling joined the business world. Doug was a part of the storytelling revival, a movement that had been gaining momentum since the 1970s and was found in performance venues, colleges, churches, conferences, and festivals. Annette had a background in advertising. She convinced Doug to help her apply stories to corporate training and leadership development; in turn, she mentored his understanding of the corporate world. Although business and political leaders had used storytelling traditions to inspire, guide, and negotiate, storytelling was an alien concept in the corporate world of the 1990s. They kept experimenting and persevering. In 1999, Doug published *Improving Your Storytelling* to help leaders develop storytelling skills. Annette published her first book, *The Story Factor*, in 2001.

Meanwhile, business storytelling has grown in breadth and depth. Story-based work has been applied to leadership, management consulting, sales, nonprofit fundraising, marketing communications, corporate communications, public relations, organization effectiveness, and change management.

Our Approach

We use the FourSight model as a foundation to describe how story techniques can enable creative collaboration. We emphasize the power of stories in visionary leadership. We also show how stories and storytelling can influence the stakeholders who sponsor, fund, and approve ideas as they advance through the innovation pipeline. Stories can accelerate innovation along two tracks:

- Fostering stakeholder support
- Inspiring creative collaboration

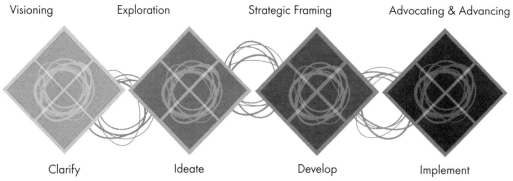

Once Upon an Innovation Framework. Adapted with permission from FourSight and the Creative Education Foundation

Our approach also integrates the strategic activities that are critical for bringing stakeholders on board. Although the framework depicts a linear approach, we see it as an iterative process that is informed by both stakeholder and team inputs.

Our View of Innovation

We embrace a broad view of innovation, and we designed this book to support a spectrum of innovation challenges—development of new products and services, process improvements, change management, plus program and curriculum design. We also consider day-to-day creative problem solving as part of innovation. We draw on a wide range of theories and approaches used during innovation and creative collaboration (e.g., design thinking, appreciative inquiry, and ethnography). These approaches inform our work, and experience tells us that stories work well with most innovation theories and models. *Once Upon an Innovation* explores a wide range of ways to weave stories into innovation.

Divergent and Convergent Thinking

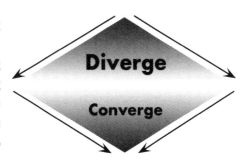

Divergent and convergent thinking are the basis for solving problems and navigating ambiguity. In his breakthrough book, *Applied Imagination*, Alex Osborn notes that divergent thinking generates a lot of ideas and options, and convergent thinking evaluates options to make decisions. A combination of the two are needed in creative problem solving. Our belief in the principles of divergent and convergent thinking connects to many of the techniques presented in this book.

Research shows that 1) more ideas produce better solutions, and 2) those who use the ground rules of divergent thinking produce twice as many good ideas as those who don't. Divergent thinking principles promote the playful and nonjudgmental mind-set required for divergent thinking. But when it's time to converge, raw ideas need to be sorted, synthesized, and evaluated using deliberate and critical thinking tools. Convergent thinking principles help a team select and refine the highest potential ideas.

Ground Rules of Divergent and Convergent Thinking

Divergent Thinking	Convergent Thinking
• Defer judgment	• Be deliberate
• Combine and build	• Check your objectives
• Seek wild ideas	• Improve your ideas
• Strive for quantity	• Be affirmative
	• Consider novelty

Navigating This Book

This book is designed as a practical and (hopefully) inspirational resource about how to use stories and storytelling not only to inspire but to accelerate innovation. Each chapter focuses on a key function related to innovation and change management. The chapters delve into how specific story techniques might enable each process. Because of the iterative and interconnected nature of this work, many theories, tools, and techniques apply to all chapters. We have cross-referenced these instances to streamline and avoid repetition.

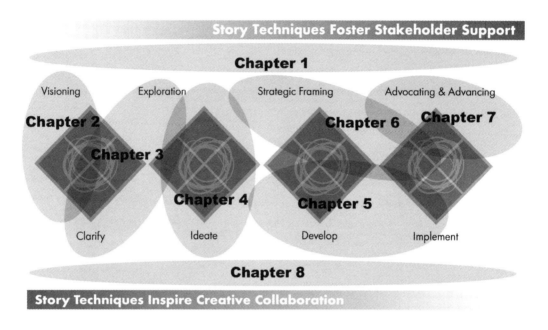

Online Tool Kit

Owners of the book can access an online tool kit with sample worksheets and templates that aid in using the techniques we present in the book. Visit onceuponinnovation.com and enter the passcode: STORYMAGIC.

Sidebars and Appendices

The book includes many sidebars with theories, examples, case studies, and exercises for readers who want to delve deeper. It also includes appendices that describe theories and methods related to innovation, creative problem solving, and business storytelling. This approach makes it easy for those familiar with the material to skip it, while still including important background for those who are new to the concepts.

Glossary

Look to the glossary for definitions of how we're deploying a number of the common terms used in business storytelling, creative problem solving, and innovation, as many of these terms have become jargon with vague or disparate meanings.

Index to Tools and Techniques

Many of the tools and techniques introduced in *Once Upon an Innovation* can be used in more than one facet of innovation. To help you strategize, we've included a useful matrix that maps out some of the many ways they can be used. It also indicates the chapter or chapters in which we discuss each technique.

Icon System

We use an icon system to make it easy to identify various types of content.

 Stories illustrate a tension or challenge one might encounter during innovation. These narratives set the stage for exploring innovation through the use of story.

 Perspectives explore various ways to use story techniques throughout the many facets of innovation. They also analyze stories to reveal deeper meanings.

 Examples highlight how stories and perspectives have been or might be applied to various business challenges. They include both hypothetical examples and case studies.

 Tools and Techniques describe processes and exercises for applying storytelling, story listening, and story structure to enhance creative collaboration.

* * * * *

We've traveled quite a distance from that initial cafeteria-booth conversation where we hatched plans for how we might merge our strengths. This book is the culmination of our collaborative journey so far. *Once Upon an Innovation* draws from our individual and shared expertise in business storytelling as a method to nurture innovation. It's a blueprint for using storytelling to facilitate change. We hope you find the insights, suggestions, and tools we provide helpful as you navigate innovation in your organization.

1
Business Storytelling Fundamentals

How to use stories in business settings

"But He Hates Me"
By Jean Storlie

In graduate school, I worked as the nutrition coordinator for an adult fitness and cardiac rehabilitation program associated with a university. As a relatively new position in the organization, it lacked established processes. Bright-eyed, naive, and optimistic, I proposed lots of new ideas to enhance and expand the nutrition services. Phil, the director, who was also my thesis advisor, would grin and say, "Jean, you can do anything you want, as long as you produce more revenue than expenses." Even though it was a nonprofit academic institution, I began to think like an entrepreneur.

While Phil supported my proposals, I experienced the opposite from Cliff, the adult fitness program manager. He resented my ideas and resisted any changes new programming would entail. At the time, I didn't understand why, and I took his naysaying way too personally. Phil ran interference, and as a result, many of my ideas came to fruition. A couple years later, when I was setting up the thesis committee for my graduate research on a new weight-control program, Phil proposed that I invite Cliff to be on the committee. In shock, I asked, "Why would I put him on my committee? He hates me!" With a twinkle in his blue eyes, Phil responded, "Well, you'll be better off with him pissing from the inside out, than the outside in."

Cliff reluctantly agreed to be included on my committee. His negativity diminished as he observed other committee members expressing enthusiasm for the program and my research. He even provided some tactical feedback, and we got along better afterward. I carried the lessons from that experience into the rest of my career.

From the Inside Out

Jean didn't realize it at the time, but Phil had paraphrazed the colorful language that Lyndon B. Johnson used when talking about his political enemies: "Better to have them inside the tent pissin' out than outside pissin' in." It stuck with her and forever changed how shes approaches innovation and project startups.

We've both worked in large organizations where getting things done requires working through a maze of stakeholders. As Jean learned early in her career, stakeholders and sponsors can enable innovation—or kill it. Jean's experience illustrates how important it is to pay attention to detractors and find ways to bring them into the process. Sometimes they convert to advocates, but their negativity is usually mitigated once they're engaged.

We believe coming up with winning ideas is only part of successful innovation. The other part is inspiring others to believe in a new idea's potential, throw their support behind it, and help execute it. Stories help both processes. This chapter builds the case for how stories can accelerate innovation and discusses how to craft a good story.

Stories Capture the Heart and Mind

A well-crafted, meaningful story can leave an audience pondering a new truth or reflecting on an old one. Innovation and creative problem solving processes involve progressive steps that weave together analytical and creative thinking as well as empathy and emotional context. Stories stimulate cognitive and emotional responses that help make sense of data.

Stories Trigger the Empathy Hormone

Not only do people like stories, but it turns out we're hardwired to respond to a good tale. Paul Zak, a leading neuroscientist, has studied the effect of storytelling on oxytocin levels. Oxytocin—also known as the love hormone—triggers feelings of compassion, trust, and empathy. Zak's work shows that the brain produces more oxytocin in response to a good story. His research also found a story needs the following narrative elements to trigger this change in brain chemistry:

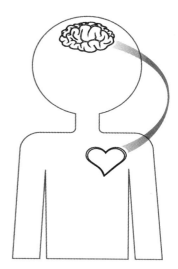

- A character (a relatable character is better)
- An obstacle, conflict, or tension (may or may not be overcome)
- A pivotal insight or moment of truth
- A journey that reveals an emotional transformation and (maybe) a universal truth

Zak's findings have an uncanny parallel to Aristotle's argument of what makes a good tragedy. Aristotle theorized that through theatrical expression of catharsis (a purging of emotion) theater makes spectators better citizens (i.e., better people). In broad terms, Aristotle argued that watching the suffering of others—their emotional transformations and discoveries—through theatrical reenactment means we don't have to repeat their errors. Perhaps Zak's scientific research supports this aesthetic theory from the fourth century BC?

Stories Can Accelerate Innovation

People light up and pay attention when you tell them a story. By harnessing the power of stories to transform how people think and feel, leaders can drive change within their organizations. Story-based leadership immerses team members in the realities and possibilities around a challenge and strengthens alignment and collaboration. Stories also lubricate how an organization adopts change.

Stories Boost Stakeholder Support

At each stage of a project's life cycle, stakeholders can endorse or quash the initiative. Strategic use of stories to engage and influence stakeholders keeps them on board. During a project launch, vision stories inspire support and help secure a green light. When checking in at key milestones, stories from the team in the trenches illuminate key insights that help stakeholders and sponsors understand challenges and potential solutions. Stories bring ideas to life, which is particularly useful when you're seeking approval to advance from concept to prototype or product development. Additionally, story structures can frame strategies and proposals into intriguing pitches.

Stories Inspire Creative Collaboration

The opening notes of the *Star Wars* anthem and gripping action scenes in the first pages of a spy novel transport us to other worlds. In magical ways, stories allow us to suspend disbelief and imagine—they take us to other places and times. Stories fuel creative collaboration by shifting energy and focus from an analytical to an imaginative mind-set.

Imaginative versus Analytical Functions

In the modern business world, many employees are assigned work that requires logical, analytical, and critical thinking, along with processing and organizing details, skills that reside mostly on the left side of the brain. These capabilities are needed to accomplish tasks and manage projects. The right side of the brain, which takes in the big picture, integrates the left brain's data and analysis within the larger situational context. The right brain turns the facts and data into patterns and possibilities. When people are overwhelmed with analytical tasks and executional demands, they have little capacity for the big-picture thinking required to generate novel ideas and solutions. Plus, a critical-thinking mind-set imposes premature judgment, which shuts down new ideas and possibilities.

Stories light up areas in the brain where metaphors, nuances, and implicit meanings are perceived. Engaging these brain pathways sheds new light on problems, which in turn enables the left-brain functions to produce unexpected and novel solutions. This response to stories parallels the phenomenon psychologists refer to as *associative thinking* (i.e., linking a thought or idea to apparently unrelated thoughts). Research shows that associative thinking, which often happens while daydreaming or allowing the mind to wander, fosters creativity.

In addition, story-based activities give teams a break from the critical thinking that can get quite intense when processing data and solving problems, especially technical problems. Our approach to story-based innovation embraces both analytical rigor and wild imagination.

Evolution of the Right-Brain, Left-Brain Theory

Beginning in the 1960s and through the 1980s, a crude model for understanding the brain's hemispheres became popular. A four-quadrant visual showed the left hemisphere as the site of reason and memory and the right as the center of emotion and imagination. This theory promoted a false assumption that everyone has a dominant brain function. You'll probably recognize the central ideas: "left-brain people are more logical and good with math and language, while right-brain people are more creative and artistic." With the advent of brain imaging and other sophisticated ways to study the brain, this theory has been debunked. But the ideas live on in pop psychology, and are embedded in management training programs and education curricula. Prolific online quizzes that score a person for their left- and right-brain dominance perpetuate the myth.

The triune brain theory, which was proposed by American neuroscientist Paul D. MacLean in the 1960s, gained momentum in the 1990s. Dave Meier's book, *The Accelerated Learning Handbook*, introduced the triune brain theory into the creative community as a way to understand how the brain responds to new ideas. It gained a large following from participants at CPSI. This model focuses on three regions of the brain:

- **Brain stem**—Houses the reptilian brain (or the *gator brain*), which controls the survival response of flight or fight (i.e., freeze, flee, or fight). The gator brain is the site of our natural human reaction to new ideas and the unknown. This hardwired instinct explains why it's hard to get participants to defer judgment when diverging.
- **Limbic system**—Surrounds the brain stem and moderates the hormones and other chemicals that affect moods such as happiness, wellness, and anxiety. The release of oxytocin in response to a good narrative is a function of the limbic system.
- **Neocortex**—Controls thinking, learning, problem solving, and creative activity in the frontal lobes of the brain. The frontal lobes are divided into right and left hemispheres, which manage similar functions in different ways and work together to perform complex cognitive tasks.

Fans of the triune brain theory use it to illuminate the significance of subconscious human emotions in decision-making. However, brain imaging studies show that this theory is oversimplified and fails to recognize the interdependence between the regions of the brain.

Neuroscience, coupled with clinical evidence from stroke victims, shows that the two brain hemispheres do the same things but in entirely different ways. The left brain focuses on details with precise and targeted attention. Like a sophisticated computer, the left brain carries out routine tasks, processes details, categorizes, and analyzes. The center for language, the left hemisphere handles reading and writing. But the left brain only sees what is explicit; it misses metaphors, imagery, and implicit meanings. The right brain, which sees the big picture, integrates the left brain's view of the world along with subtleties in a larger context. The right brain sees nuances and understands metaphors, humor, and subjective reality.

The rapidly evolving field of neuroscience continues to discover new complexities of the human brain, which is why simplistic models don't hold up. We believe the whole brain comes into play during creative thinking, which is at the heart of storytelling. Stories fire up parts of the brain where emotion, imagination, and creativity occur—areas of the brain that are underused in the modern workplace.

Stories Shape Culture and Facilitate Change

Innovation and change management go hand in hand. Innovation leaders need to manage both the process of developing new products and solutions and the organization's capacity to adopt and support fledgling opportunities. Sometimes a company's norms enable innovation; other times they stifle it. Management guru Peter Drucker wrote, "Culture eats strategy for breakfast." This often-cited quote crystallizes a widespread belief among business leaders and consultants that the preexisting culture of a company can thwart a winning strategy and innovation. Simply put, if an organization's culture resists innovation and fights to maintain the status quo, the best strategies and ideas will fail.

An organization's culture is reflected in the stories employees tell about their workplace. If the stories are good, the culture is probably healthy; bad stories signal a dysfunctional culture. Listening to employee stories will help a leader understand the culture—plus, storytelling tools offer powerful ways to change the culture.

Innovation often brings change that ripples across an organization, extending beyond the function, product, or system that's intended to change. When innovation disrupts established systems and norms, other employees will be affected and some may resent having to adjust their work flow and processes. For example, Jean's nutrition and weight-control programs disrupted the adult-fitness operations. That became a source of irritation to Cliff, so he undermined the program. Taking time to understand the effects of innovation on other people's work and bring them on board is a critical step. When employees embrace the vision behind an innovation, they will work to help it succeed. In addition to other stakeholder management tools, stories can help others imagine the future potential of an idea or innovation and see its value.

For all these reasons, it's not a surprise that story techniques are gaining traction in the organizational effectiveness and change-management communities as an approach to reshaping the culture.

Stories in Organizational Change

Helen Kuyper, a global leader in change management who is based in Ireland, defines culture as the "collective mind-set of an organization." She uses stories to facilitate change in organizations. Kuyper believes the first step in changing the collective mind-set is listening to employees' stories to identify what's really going on in an organization. She works with senior leaders to process the employees' stories and create a vision for change. Then she uses story-sharing exercises to engage groups of employees to co-create a new, collective story inspired by the leaders' vision for change. She asserts that when employees are coauthors of the change story, they adopt a new mind-set that propels organizational change.

1-2-3 Steps to Craft a Good Story

You can extract stories from books, fables, and fairy tales, but there is nothing like a true story to get people to sit up and pay attention. One way to become a storyteller is to curate episodes from your life and turn them into stories that apply to business situations. When crafting stories about objects, like a brand, product, or technology, "the story" might be harder to find. But it's not impossible.

Look for a human angle about the "thing." Are there founders, leaders, or employees whose stories paint a picture? Or is there a community or higher purpose served? You can also gather user stories about the real-life experiences of people who consume or buy a product or service. User stories help innovation teams gain empathy for their customers and obtain feedback on what works and doesn't work in users' lives.

As a beginning point to storytelling, we offer a three-step approach to turn episodes from your own life and the people you've observed into meaningful narratives for professional communications:

1. Discover story gems
2. Develop plot and meaning
3. Polish with salient details

Step 1: Discover Story Gems

Everyone's life contains a treasure trove of experiences that can be turned into stories for professional and personal communications. Get started by finding your *story gems*—raw ideas that have potential to become a story. Your goal in this first phase is unearthing a variety of story gems and then examining them to find their deeper meaning and potential applications. The Mining for Stories tool can help you recall stories out of your experiences and examine if they might illuminate a leadership or business situation.

Mine for Stories

To get started, skim through the story prompts listed in the left column to see if any of them spark a memory. Meander through the four rows (people, place, events, and objects) to uncover as many story gems as you can. At this point, don't worry about capturing the whole story—just the essence of it. We've sketched out how the "He Hates Me Story," might be developed with this tool. Visit onceuponinnovation.com to download a worksheet to mine your life for stories.

	Pathways to Explore	Find Your Story Gems	Find the Deeper Meaning	Link to Your Work
People	• Teacher you'll never forget • Boss who gave harsh feedback • Loyal friend • Colorful roommate • Someone you hero-worshipped	But He Hates Me? Better to have him piss from the inside out	Engage resisters during innovation	Resisters can impede success Resisters provide criticism that strengthens ideas
Places	• Favorite places • Unfamiliar or scary places • Mountains and oceans			
Events	• Flunking your driver's test • Interviewing for first job • Leaving for college • Narrowly escaping a disaster • Meeting your spouse			
Objects	• First car • Favorite food • Something you lost or broke • Cherished gift • Frivolous purchase			

Explore the Deeper Meaning

Pick a story gem and examine it from different angles to extract its meaning. Reflect on the various meanings your story might convey—many stories have more than one. That's fine. Jot them all down. Here are some thought starters:

- Core value
- Lesson you learned
- Mistake you made
- People who shaped your life
- Where you find comfort or satisfaction
- How you overcame a challenge

Find Connection to Work

Many great stories can be applied to business situations, but not all of them. Ponder how the meaning or message you've just identified might apply to your work. Curate personal stories that can spice up a presentation, coach an employee, or convey your leadership values. Explore the following story themes to see if you can find a resonant story:

- Conjuring your favorite place could set the tone for a warm, welcoming kickoff to a team event
- Getting lost in the woods could provide lessons for innovation or problem solving
- Losing your luggage in a foreign airport could reveal how to cope with a communication barrier

Story gems often tumble out when talking to friends over coffee, chatting with family members around the dinner table, or when randomly bumping into colleagues in the hallway. Collect these gems by writing down a few key words to jog your memory so they can be retrieved and polished later.

Step 2: Develop Plot and Meaning

When listeners travel with your characters through a struggle—even if the obstacle is not overcome—they experience the same pivotal insights and emotional transformation. If you tease out important narrative elements, your stories stand a better chance of connecting with your audience. While it's not the only way to develop a plot, the classic narrative arc provides a way to begin crafting stories. Derivations of this framework might involve flashbacks, subplots, or skipping over some plot points to let listeners use their imaginations to fill in the blanks. These dramatic techniques run the risk of making your story confusing, long, or too corny, so don't overdo it with plot twists from the main story.

Plot: The Backbone of a Story

How you structure your story can increase—or decrease—its impact. Many novice (and natural) storytellers meander into irrelevant details during the setup and rising tension, causing audiences to get lost, get distracted, or lose interest. In business settings, you need to grab their attention, get to the point, and tell your tale in a couple minutes. Distilling a story to its essence is key.

As you balance brevity with emotional impact and clarity, it can be helpful to visualize the storyline. The Plot Your Story template, based on the classic narrative arc, provides a framework to sketch out the story structure.

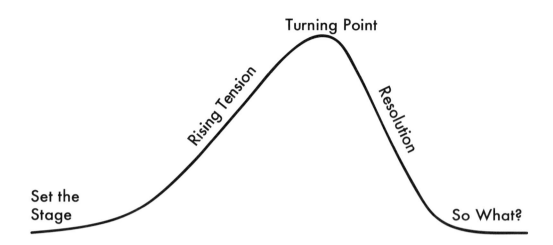

The Situation / Setup

Reveal the core essence of the situation with an attention-grabbing hook. Consider starting with a conversation, inner dialogue, memory, or evocative setting to establish the tone. A cherished axiom of journalism is "Show, don't tell." Your introduction should grab your audience's attention while providing context and essential details, like who the characters are, where they are, and what's happening. Use vivid sensory details, but be concise. Audiences lose interest during rambling introductions.

Tension-Building Plot Points

How many times have you listened to someone recite an episode by walking through what happened in sequential detail (first this, then that, and then, and then, and then . . .)? Many of us fall into that common pitfall when recounting something that happened. Use the Plot Your Story template to outline a story, sketching out key plot points that build tension and create intrigue. Many emerging storytellers try to cram too many sequential details into the left side of the arc. As a rule of thumb, aim for two to four plot points or events that build anxiety, tension, drama, and intensity. Strip away unnecessary details—while they may be important to you, chances are the audience doesn't care, and they might be distracting or confusing.

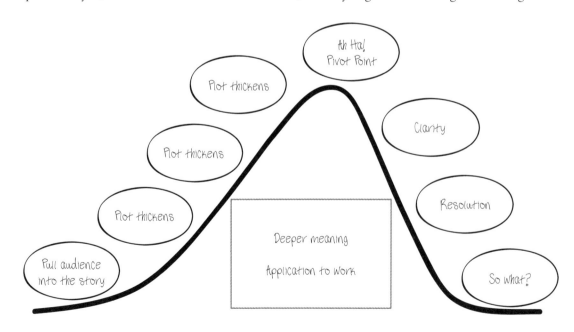

The Pivot Point

This crucial moment in a story goes by many names, such as *turning point, climax, or moment of truth*. A character may experience a realization, or another character might shed new light on the situation that changes the path forward. The struggle may not necessarily be resolved at this point, but after this moment, the character sees the situation in a different way and is changed. Punctuate this pivotal moment. If you're verbally sharing the story, consider using a long pause, hand gesture, facial expression, shift in stance, or movement to emphasize this moment.

Land the Story

After the pivot point, the pieces of the puzzle fall into place. No need to belabor all the implications, but share a couple of outcomes that illustrate how the situation has changed and the struggle was resolved. Your goal is to land your story and lead the audience to the final "So what?"

"So What?"

Close the story by extracting a larger truth or meaning that can be applied to other situations. Ask yourself: So what is the point of this story? How did this experience change the character's viewpoint, circumstances, relationship(s), or life? The change may be simple or profound. How might you illuminate the conclusion(s)? Sometimes the character's turning point reflects a universal truth, or relatable human experience.

"But He Hates Me" Plot Analysis

Take a look at how the story, "But He Hates Me," can be sketched out using the Plot Your Story template. Note especially how key plot points along the narrative arc are identified. If you go back to the opening story of this chapter, you'll notice it includes more details that bring the plot to life, but the overall structure can be distilled down to a few key plot points.

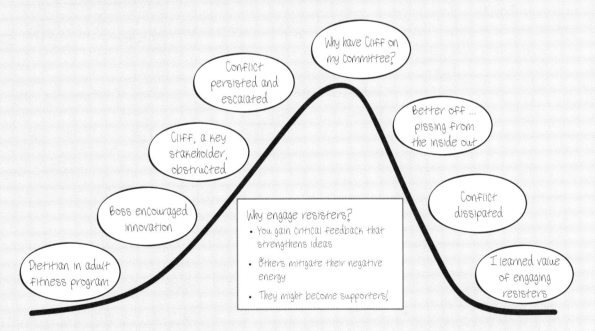

Extract Meaning

Go deeper into the emotional elements of the story. While sketching out story lines, we like to capture the deeper meaning in the space underneath the arc. When you're extracting the deeper meaning, consider how the character(s) transitioned to a new point of view and what others can learn from it. As illustrated in the "But He Hates Me" plot analysis, Jean learned the value of including resisters in the innovation process:

- Resisters provide critical input that strengthens ideas. Learning about the problems and flaws early in the process can head off bigger problems later.
- Involving resisters can dissipate their negativity. When they're part of a larger stakeholder team, resisters have a forum for venting their criticisms and their resistance often becomes more manageable.
- Resisters might become supporters. Not always, but if they have skin in the game, they start to support and advocate. It's magical when that happens!

Think about life lessons that might be extracted from your stories. A story that conveys triumph over adversity might inspire a path forward for an innovation team or give a discouraged employee hope. A story about team dynamics leading to success or failure might help a group change their norms. Stories about relationships illuminate team dynamics and help leaders address obvious but unspoken challenges. Your story gems might reveal:

- Leadership values
- Hard lessons learned
- Empathy for alternative perspectives
- Insight into a user experience
- Value of personal connections

Explore Perspectives

It can be helpful to explore story gems from different perspectives by gathering stories from others involved in the same experience (e.g., stakeholders, team members, or users). Convene a story circle or interview them to learn their stories and viewpoints. Consider all these viewpoints as you extract meaning—sometimes they have a shared experience, sometimes each character in a story has a different experience of the same events. In chapter 5, we'll explore how to identify the best voice or point of view from which to tell your story.

Universal Plots

- The Quest
- The Heroic Act
- The Threat Among Us
- Fish Out of Water
- Impossible Odds
- Speaking Truth to Power
- The Noble Stand
- Virtue Rewarded at Last
- Rite of Passage
- Overcoming a Fatal Flaw
- Journey to the Heart
- Redemption
- The Point of No Return
- Dream Comes True
- The Lonely Path of the Visionary
- The Enigma

Connect Your Story to a Universal Plot

We recommend spending some time with David Hutchens's *Circle of the 9 Muses*, which is rich with salient ideas and helpful insights. He advises business storytellers to consider pinning their stories to universal plots. He devotes a chapter to defining and mapping a number of plots alongside examples from movies and literature, and connecting those universal plots to various business situations.

For example, he calls our attention to the beginning of the Harry Potter series. Harry's arrival at Hogwarts is built on the Fish Out of Water plot, in which a character (1) finds himself in a fascinating place where the rules are different, (2) discovers what used to work before doesn't work here, (3) has to learn new skills, behaviors, and improvise, (4) navigates through the situation, and (5) changes and grows from this challenge, becoming more aware and resilient. Most of us feel like a fish out of water when starting a new job or getting a promotion. Business teams feel the same when pushing innovation into new regions of the world, new categories, and new technologies.

Step 3: Polish with Salient Details

Vivid language brings characters and setting to life for the audience. The final step in developing a story is to incorporate sensory details to describe people, places, and events. We open with a simple story that illustrates the importance of including salient details.

"I Saw the Deer and Shot It"

My husband's Grandpa Bill was a master storyteller. He owned a newspaper and told stories for a living, but he also created a storytelling culture in their family—at the dinner table, around the campfire, and as part of family events. A favorite time for storytelling was when they gathered during deer-hunting season and shared tales of the hunt. One year, my husband's brother, Harry, who was about fourteen at the time, had bagged the prize deer, so Grandpa Bill turned to him in the midst of their Thanksgiving feast and asked him to tell his story. Startled, Harry looked up from his plate and said, "I saw the deer and shot it."

After a brief and somewhat awkward pause, Grandpa Bill looked at him and affectionately said, "Harry, you may now retire to the bedroom and practice telling that story. You might want to think about where you were, the movements of the deer, the wind direction, how you took aim, the length of the shot. We'll be waiting for you to try again."

— Jean Storlie

The Goldilocks Principle

Stripped of intrigue and sensory details, Harry's story lacked essential narrative elements, and it fell flat. Grandpa Bill's coaching is great advice on how to tell better stories. Details that evoke images, smells, and sounds bring the listener into your story and make them feel like they were there. Depicting how characters and events collide in a tension or drama creates suspense that captivates audiences. Some colorful or bizarre details make the story memorable. But, at the other end of the spectrum, too many details and tangents can bore and confuse your listeners. Striking the right balance is the art of storytelling.

Bring Characters and Scenes to Life

Notice that Grandpa Bill's advice was to add salient details that evoke all five senses. Most people default to visual descriptions of people and situations. Stir your audience's imagination by including sound, smell, taste, and touch. Let's say you wanted to describe an obnoxious man who was rude to you. "Cheap cologne burned my throat as he stepped in front of me and blocked my view of the parade. His spittle sprayed my face as he turned to holler 'Over here!' to his buddies, motioning them to wedge into the space." These two sentences convey the smell, sound, and behavior of a character, as well as the scene where the story takes place.

Vivid Language Example

Look for use of vivid descriptions in the following essay written by a teenage girl who tells the story about flunking her driver's test. How do these passages convey the girl's emotions? Can you empathize with her experience? Does this give you insights into how teenage girls view the world? What other passages grab at your heartstrings?

"Sour Sixteenth Birthday"

The ticktock of the clock echoed in my ears with each passing second. I'd been silently reciting driving rules like a broken record. It was my sixteenth birthday. At 12:45, my dad picked me up from school and took me to the DMV to take my drivers test. Anxiety surged through my body like an electrical current when I handed the administrator my paperwork. As we waited for my appointment to start, I took deep breaths to calm my nerves while my dad quizzed me. I was prepared!

After twenty restless minutes, a scowling woman with a tragic hairdo approached my car. I silently begged for her to walk past, but she knocked on my window to signal that she would be conducting my test. I felt her disapproval itch my skin. When she lowered herself into the passenger seat, the trace of her cheap perfume stung my nostrils. Her eyes pierced through me with a dismissive cynicism when I introduced myself in my most cheery and respectful manner. She mumbled *hello* as she shuffled through her papers.

Thoughts flashed through my brain faster than I could register them. It was all I could do to focus on her commands: "Next left ... Right ahead ..." A few minutes into the test, we approached a T-intersection, and she instructed me to turn left. "So far, so good," I thought as I eased toward the intersection. There was no stop sign, so I checked both ways for traffic. But I could not see to the right, so I slowly released my foot from the brake and inched forward for a better view. Just when I could see the intersection, she jutted her arm in front of my chest and shrieked, "There's a bus!"

I slammed on the brakes. My heart raced. I couldn't speak. It felt like days passed before she said, "That was bad. That was really bad." In that moment, my confidence evaporated. A wave of tears nearly overflowed my eyes, and a painful ache crawled down my throat. I'd barely started the test and already ruined my chances of passing!

When we were done, she sighed, "Well, you'll have to come back next week." My disappointment poisoned the air as I breathed heavily and attempted to suppress my tears. She'd just crushed my only birthday wish. Even though I'd expected this outcome the minute she slid into the car, my dreams of teenage independence were shattered. At least temporarily.

—Eleanor Harkness, Jean's daughter

Practice Evocative Language Using All Five Senses

Here's an exercise to help you practice describing characters and scenes through all five senses. Your description of a setting is more robust when you go beyond visual descriptors. Then take the experiment further by isolating one or two senses as you describe a situation or place—this helps you go deeper into your sensory experience.

It's often helpful to close your eyes, slow your breath, and tune into your breathing cycle as you do these exercises. Count to five during each inhalation and exhalation. Cycle through a few breaths before reflecting on these prompts.

- *Beach vacation*—Imagine you're on an ocean beach. Take in the view, and then think about the sounds, smells, tastes, and touches in that setting.
- *Fall walk in the woods*—Take a mental walk through the woods on a glorious fall day. Describe the colors and light, the smells, and the sound of leaves crunching, as well as the sensations of the sun and crisp air on your skin.
- *Winter walk*—Conjure a winter scene and focus only on the sounds you hear. "Crunch. Crunch. Crunch. Like styrofoam, the snow squeaks with each footstep."
- *Holiday tastes*—Describe a holiday through the smells and tastes you associate with it. Do these memories produce vivid descriptions of food, family, and friends?
- *Wind on your skin*—Contrast these two descriptions of how the wind might feel. "The wind slapped my face as I stepped onto Michigan Avenue on a windy Chicago day." "As I lounged in the hammock, a gentle breeze soothed my sunburned skin and lulled me to sleep." Notice how these descriptions evoke very different scenes.

Guided Imagery

When facilitating a group, guided imagery can be used to cue participants through these exercises. This allows them to focus on their breathing and memories, which takes them into a deeper meditative state. We like to demonstrate the technique by inviting participants to envision a mini-vacation to their favorite place. It's an easy starting point for this more imaginative exploration. Chapter 2 contains how-to guidance on the Guided Imagery technique.

Closing Thoughts

Stories alone don't produce innovation, but they do stimulate regions of the brain needed for complex cognitive tasks and creative thinking. Good stories leave others with a lasting impression that can persuade or influence them long after the initial telling.

The magic lies in how good stories trigger the release of oxytocin, the empathy hormone. But getting to that magical effect takes more than saying, "I'm going to tell you a story . . . " Narratives that prompt the brain to produce oxytocin tend to include at least one character, a struggle, a moment of truth, and an emotional transition. A good story well told brings listeners along with the characters on their journey. The listener feels what the characters feel and is touched emotionally.

Building skills in storytelling can help innovators and change-leaders bring others through the ambiguous and complex process of producing an innovation. In the opening story, Jean learned how stakeholders can make or break innovation. The power of stories to bring people into an imaginative state of mind helps both inventors and stakeholders consider possibilities rather than obstacles. Storytelling is an influence skill that can be pulled out at a moment's notice once you've collected a treasure chest of story gems and know how to craft and polish your stories.

The three-step process introduced in this chapter helps you craft stories that can be used throughout the innovation process. The first step is discovering your own story gems by mining your experiences for episodes that could become meaningful, relevant stories. Then you polish those gems by developing the plot and meaning, using the classic narrative arc as a simple tool for outlining the story. And finally, you add sensory details to describe characters and settings with vivid language.

Upcoming chapters apply these business storytelling fundamentals to various aspects of innovation and creative problem solving. Return to the tools discussed in this chapter as you create stories to lead innovation and change in your organization. The principles of good storytelling will serve you well in personal and business situations.

Telling a story is like building a castle rather than a line in the sand.
—Annette Simmons

2
Storytelling in Visioning

Stories help people imagine a future state

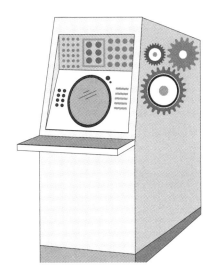

"Why Does a Jock School Need a Computer?"
By Jean Storlie

My dad fumed as he left a meeting with the University of Wisconsin Board of Regents. It was the early 1960s, and he had just pitched a proposal for the University of Wisconsin-La Crosse (UWL) to install a computer system. Not only had they dismissed him, one regent scoffed, "Computers? Aren't those gadgets that physicists at Madison play with? Why does a jock school need a computer!?" (UWL was known for its physical education department.)

But John "Jack" Storlie didn't give up. He returned to campus, where he was an assistant professor of chemistry, and continued to evangelize for computers. After completing a summer course in computer programming on a study grant from the National Science Foundation, he was a convert.

Jack roamed the halls of campus, talking about computers. He frequently ranted in the faculty lounge about the regents' lack of vision. One day, a colleague who studied kinesiology started a conversation about how to use computers for the extensive numerical analyses required for motion studies. They applied for a grant to conduct a performance study on the university's football players. They were awarded the funds and published the results.

Jack kept pitching two computers—one for administration and another for academics—because the administrative needs were so vast. When he described a future workplace with computer terminals on everyone's desk, the administrators laughed, "Secretaries? Why would secretaries need computers?"

When Jack returned to the Board of Regents a few years later, he began, "The last time I was here, you asked what a 'jock school' could do with a computer." He passed out the article. "This motion study, which was enabled by a computer, helped UWL win football games." His stories about how computers could transform not just UWL but every university helped convince them to install two mainframes.

In 1968, Jack abandoned the chemistry classroom to lead both the academic and administrative computing programs. Upon celebrating its fiftieth anniversary in 2018, UWL's Computer Science Department boasted 312 majors, 46 minors, and 28 graduate students in that year. And a processing capacity far beyond those first two mainframes Jack fought to secure.

Archetype of a Visionary

Jack's battle with the University of Wisconsin regents reflects the archetype of the lonely visionary who is driven by a dream but encounters critics who throw up barriers. The story mirrors David Hutchens's outline of the universal plot of the visionary who makes sacrifices to unveil a creation. Whether they're met with acclaim or derision, the world is changed because of the visionary. Eventually the visionary is recognized, fulfilled, and rewarded—sometimes not until many years later. The accompanying illustration shows how Jack's story parallels the universal plot "The Lonely Path of a Visionary."

The Lonely Path of the Visionary

Visionary was driven by a vision to do something new	Encountered critics, who couldn't see the vision, and faced barriers	Made sacrifices alone for what he or she believed in	Unveiled a brilliant creation (to acclaim or derision)	Today the world is improved because of the visionary, who is fulfilled and recognized

Why Does a Jock School Need a Computer?

Jack saw how computers could revolutionize academic research and administration	Regents shot him down; people scoffed at his view of the future workplace	Jack put his reputation at risk; he lost time with his family	Jack got two mainframes installed; he was promoted	UW-L computer science progran celebrated 50 years and honored Jack

Inspired by the graphic that appears in *Circle of the Nine Muses* by David Hutchens. Used with permission.

Visionaries come off as bold and a little crazy because they see a future the rest of us find preposterous. Jack imagined a future where computers would transform everyday life at the university. Even when no one believed his forecast that everyone would need computers on their desks, he kept pushing for two mainframes. He helped people across the campus envision how they could be a part of the change. When others see *your* vision as *their* vision, innovation gets traction.

To fully embrace the future he worked so hard to achieve, Jack hit a turning point where he had to make the hard choice to leave his vocation as a chemistry professor. He always missed the classroom, but the bigger dream of computers swept him into the whirlwind of change. Visionaries often face a moment when they have to let go of the past to live in the future they created. Keep in mind that this archetypal story plays out in large and small ways in companies and organizations when visionaries push for change.

This chapter explores how visionaries, innovators, and change makers can use stories to bring others along. The archetype of a visionary provides valuable lessons for these bold leaders and others in an organization who sponsor and follow their efforts. Keeping this context in mind, we move on to explore how stories can help craft a vision, explore it with a team, and translate it into action.

Craft the Vision

Knowledge, logic, and analysis help ground a vision in reality and build a plan, but inspiring a vision requires passion. Whether you're crafting a vision alone or with a team, discovery processes that move back and forth between analytical and creative thinking are needed when forming a vision.

Stories tap into the heart and mind—and simultaneously foster connections between the two. Stories can help a leader discover and articulate a vision. To ground your vision in a story, find a compelling tale that helps people imagine a future where this vision becomes reality. Engage key contributors in processes that help them imagine the future in a way that is different than today. A company story might be an evocative choice—for example, the organization's origin story or a key turning point in its development. Or seek inspiration from a metaphor, movie, or fable.

Explore the Vision with the Team

Sometimes it's hard to get others to buy into a future that's dramatically different than today's reality (e.g., Jack's critics scoffing, "Why would secretaries need computers?"). Visionary leaders tell great stories that overcome the obstacles by conveying their dreams in ways that help others imagine new possibilities and get inspired to be a part of them. Martin Luther King Jr.'s 1963 "I Have a Dream" speech envisions a future in which a new, harmonious, and equal existence is possible. John F. Kennedy's moon-shot speech in 1962 told a story of triumph, heroism, and impossible dreams.

To get a team inspired about a leader's vision, facilitated sessions can help the leader and team collaborate to translate his or her vision into a shared narrative and action plan. The success of these sessions hinges on how well leaders articulate their visions during the kickoff. Passionate language with stories of hope and opportunity help people believe. Belief ignites action.

Translate the Vision into Action

Just as Jack helped his colleagues understand how computers could change their day-to-day lives, think about how you might invite stakeholders into your vision. How might different stakeholders respond to transformational possibilities? Some will respond to financial visions of success; others will care more about customer experience, productivity, or employee satisfaction.

A leader's vision radiates through an organization. Successful visionaries share an inspiring new plan for the future, which helps others adopt a receptive mind-set. And their newly opened mind-set galvanizes behavioral change. Visionaries provoke behaviors that foster the called-for change, and they respectfully discourage actions that inhibit it.

In fostering a change-enabling mind-set, imagine how each stakeholder might benefit (or lose). Be empathetic about their motives and share your vision in light of what it means for them. Understand that some may feel threatened by change in general and the proposed change in particular. Use stories to help them try on a new mind-set that aligns with the envisioned change. Tap into the power of stories to encourage people to believe. Invent stories about what people would be saying and doing if the vision became reality.

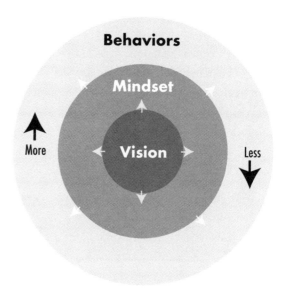

Work with the team to identify behaviors the organization will experience more of if the vision becomes reality. Provide illustrative stories or invite team members to create ones that provide glimpses into what it will be like when the vision comes true. Reinforce behaviors that enable the vision to become reality and discourage those that block it. In addition to engaging team members in turning a vision into action, leaders can use this approach to bring stakeholders on board. (Chapter 7 provides a tool for analyzing stakeholders' stories.)

Turn the ideas, input, and stories you learn from interacting with stakeholders and team members into goals and action steps toward the proposed vision. Add tactics, timelines, and assignments to develop a concrete plan to guide the way.

Case Study: 2020 Vision Story

"When Women Dream"

Morning sun lit the spacious conference room as women leaders gathered to develop a "2020 Vision." It was 2010, and the director of diversity and inclusion at General Mills had convened thirty women leaders who represented all the company's functions. She also hired a facilitator, Linda, who would help the team imagine possibilities by sharing their "career-best" stories. A genuine and relatable facilitator, Linda was trained in appreciative inquiry and knew the company and some of the participants.

The women convened for warm-up activities around a U-shaped table in a room spacious enough for them to roam and mingle as well. After breaking the ice, the participants worked independently to describe a career-best experience. After some individual reflection, Linda guided participants to pair up and share their stories. Each pair then partnered with another pair to share their stories and identify themes. The foursomes became eightsomes, and these larger groups continued to share and build. The energy mounted as participants discovered common experiences through their career-best stories.

Eventually the entire gathering merged their stories into a shared narrative of what the company could achieve "if every employee experienced more career bests." The women gathered around the table again and crafted a vision and strategic framework in the last session of the workshop.

I've never witnessed a strategy come together so seamlessly and collaboratively. Even the (often painful) step of drafting the language for the vision and four strategic pillars was harmonious and inspiring.

Furthermore, the original language stuck through a rigorous series of stakeholder input sessions that followed. The company executives supported the strategy, and the women of the leadership council rallied behind the slogan, "By women. For everyone." The strategic pillars turned into action plans, and women collaborated across functional boundaries to promote a career-best culture in which everyone brings their best to work every day.

Ten years later, General Mills credits the 2020 Vision and the advocacy of women for their industry-leading parental leave policy that began in 2018. The Boundaryless Work pillar inspired a program that supports employees to manage their careers through lateral growth opportunities, turning a traditional career ladder into a career lattice. The company also engages the global women's community in an annual event on International Women's Day.

—Jean Storlie

Leverage women to drive championship results

By women. For everyone.

Equal Voice Everywhere	Global Women's Community	Boundaryless Work	Platinum Culture

General Mills' 2020 "Women in Leadership" Vision & Strategy. Used with permission.

The Blind Men and the Elephant

In the 2018 issue of *Cereal Foods World*, an applied scientific publication, guest editors Padu Krishnan and Wayne Moore share the parable of the blind men and the elephant to illustrate the concept that data can be misleading when examined in isolation. Through this tactile, easily imagined parable, they challenged their colleagues to reconsider how they interpret and process data. In the parable, which originated in India, a group of blind men who've never before encountered an elephant learn and conceptualize what the elephant is like by touching it.

> Each blind man feels a different part of the elephant's body, but only one part, such as the side or the tusk. They each describe the elephant based on their partial experience and their descriptions are in complete disagreement on what an elephant is. In some versions, they suspect that another person is dishonest and they come to blows. The moral of the parable is that humans have a tendency to project their partial experiences as the whole truth and ignore other people's related experiences; instead, people should consider that they may be partially right and that others may possess useful information that reveals the whole truth.

Imagining through Stories

- Create a shared vision among stakeholders and the core team
- Identify employee stories that link to a leader's vision
- Translate a leader's vision into a story that motivates others

Story Techniques for Visioning

The 2020 Vision case study illustrates how a shared vision for organizational change was developed through the appreciative inquiry technique, which starts with participants sharing stories about a "best" experience, in this case, a career best. Using their career-best stories as a foundation, participants imagined their workplace ten years into the future. They dreamed of a workplace where women leaders would represent half the executive leadership team. They imagined a time when women's leadership skills and values are integrated into the culture.

Just as the appreciative inquiry-inspired stories helped these women imagine a future state and articulate it for others, many other story-based techniques help teams identify, clarify, and articulate a vision. We compiled a few of our favorites.

Snowball Pair and Share

The 2020 Vision example also used the Snowball Pair and Share technique to merge common elements of individual stories into a powerful shared narrative. The exercise involves a series of rounds, in which participants (beginning with pairs) share stories and find common themes. The initial pairs join with other pairs to become groups of four, and then eight, and so on—becoming successively larger groups and communities.

During the process, participants capture common elements of individual stories using flip charts, sticky notes, or worksheets. Eventually, the team creates a collective story that represents their shared experience. This story forms their rallying call and ignites action around the vision. Sometimes a singular theme or story emerges, but more often two to four overarching themes or stories rise to the top. Referring to archetypes and universal plots might help the team understand and articulate these shared stories

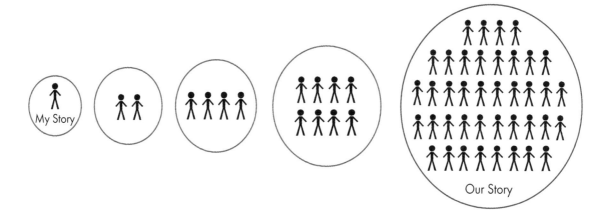

Appreciative Inquiry

Appreciative inquiry (AI) is an organizational-change model with a large global following. It engages stakeholders in story-based activities to mobilize change through a four-stage process: discover, dream, design, and deliver. AI starts by eliciting stories about positive experiences related to the opportunity or goal through an interview process about an affirmative topic (strategic issue framed in a positive context). These stories help teams generate a shared vision and direct their energy toward positive change. AI focuses on identifying what's already working well, analyzing why, and then encouraging more positive behaviors and initiatives. Basic tenets of AI are that an organization will grow in whichever direction the people in the organization focus their attention; stories illuminate where their energy is going. AI isn't entirely based in stories, but it intersects with business storytelling in a meaningful way.

The first stage of AI, *discovery*, employs story-based practices, where stakeholders interview each other and share stories about "best-of" experiences. The story-sharing experience helps build relationships, find common ground, and create a shared narrative about the desired future state. To illustrate, a story prompt in AI might begin, "Tell me a story about your best-ever experience buying a car"—or another experience associated with the vision or challenge being addressed.

The 2020 Vision story reveals how an AI process was experienced by members of a team who were developing a ten-year vision. When participants unearthed their career-best stories and shared them with others through a Snowball Pair and Share exercise, the group found remarkable commonalities through their career-best stories. That allowed them to collectively envision a future state and identify key strategies to achieve this vision. The thirty participants became advocates who went back and spread the word throughout all levels of the organization. Look to appendix B for more background on the AI technique.

Metaphor-Based Activities

Before leaders can create a shared vision, they need to first identify and articulate their own ideal future. This isn't always easy; inspiration of some sort can be immensely helpful. This is where the magical combination of metaphor and story can be your crystal ball. Metaphorical thinking is a substitutional mental process in which implicit comparisons are made between qualities of objects that are usually considered in separate classifications. Trying to understand things through logic alone disrupts the creative process. Metaphorical thinking is a powerful tool for looking at things in a new way—including a vision.

Photo Metaphors

Collect twenty to thirty images for this exercise. You can use photos related to a theme that connects to the challenge or vision, a random collection of images, or a blend. Find images in your photo collection, purchase stock images, print free internet images, or clip pictures from magazines. You can also buy an innovation photo deck. ("PicTour Imagine" from Sherlock Creative Thinking is a great tool for this exercise. You can order it at sherlockcreativethinking.com.) Spread the images out on a floor, table, or wall with plenty of room for participants to roam around and see each picture clearly. Have participants go "photo shopping" to find a picture that represents their ideal future. Encourage the photo shoppers to quickly choose a picture that resonates with them for any reason without overthinking their selection. Next, have each person tell a story about the picture they chose and how it expresses their vision. If you're working with a large group, you can have participants process their picture stories in pairs or small groups to save time. Consider some of the following variations on this technique or come up with your own.

Wide Angle

Have participants select two pictures: one that represents the current state and another that represents the future. Give them time to write or draw a story that illuminates how to make the vision become a reality. You can also put two random pictures into envelopes and have each person develop a vision story from these forced connections.

Museum Gallery Tour

Post pictures on walls or mobile poster boards. Create a museum ambiance with lighting and music. Have participants take notes and sketches to capture inspiring images that evoke their vision. They can then return to their seats and write or draw a vision story.

Safari Photo Tour

Have participants use their smartphones to take photos of the pictures they find most inspiring. They can then use their photos to craft a vision story using digital tools.

Scavenger Hunt

Give each participant a clue or insight related to the challenge. Have participants search for an image that relates in some way to their clue. They can then take that picture back to their seat and write a vision story inspired by connecting their clue to the picture they chose.

Physical Metaphors

Physical objects can be used instead of pictures as described above in the Photo Metaphor activity. Gather a random collection of objects, like toys, tools, cooking utensils, household items, relics from nature, mementos, and anything else you can find. For a gallery-like experience, display the objects for participants to peruse and select the object that symbolizes the vision as they see it. Alternatively, have them blindly select an object from a bag and engage in a forced-connection exercise to describe the future.

Build a Metaphor

Unlike using an existing image or object as a metaphor, participants can build their own metaphors. Instruct them to build 3-D models of a desired future state within a very short time period, typically three to five minutes. Encourage participants to dive into the building process and keep building the entire time without thinking or deliberating too much, forcing their imaginations to become tangible. When time is called, ask participants to tell a spontaneous story about what they built.

During a debrief after the extemporaneous stories, have the creator explain each element of the structure, why it was included, and what it represents. Encourage the group to ask questions about the physical structure, probing for deeper meanings. Through this discussion, the metaphors represented by each physical object come into focus. When used with groups, a vision emerges from the commonalities in the stories.

The combination of hands-on, imaginative play and spontaneous storytelling unlocks innovative thinking. Many variations are possible with this technique by combining different building materials with different story-sharing formats. Consider the following options to mix and match building materials with story-sharing activities.

Hands-On Building/Crafting Materials	Story-Sharing Activities
• LEGOs	• Spontaneous story sharing
• Tinkertoys	• Campfire story circles
• Magnetic building-block sets	• Poems and six-word stories
• Craft supplies (pipe cleaners, clay, etc.)	• Anecdote circles
• Costumes	• Story writing
• Office or party supplies (paper clips, sticky notes, balloons, etc.)	• Narrative-arc templates
	• Skits or thirty-second advertising spots

Guided Imagery

Breathing exercises can transform a group's collective energy and tap into creative energy. The use of yoga-like breathing along with a set of cues can help teams look to the future in a more imaginative state of mind. Invite participants to imagine being in a story about what the future looks like when [the vision] becomes reality. In quiet reflection after the guided imagery, have participants write or draw their story. You might phrase a writing prompt in this vein: "Let's imagine five years from now, the organization has achieved [the vision]. Tell me a story about what it looks like for [you, consumers, employees, the company, the world]?"

- Close your eyes and sit in a comfortable, neutral position: feet flat, arms resting gently on your knees. Take a cleansing breath.
- Focus on your breath. Slow it down, breathing deeply on both inhales and exhales.
- Imagine you're in a future ideal place. (Refine this cue based on the vision you're pursuing.)
- With each breath imagine the details of the space around you. What do you see? What do you hear? What do you smell? What do you taste? What do you feel and touch? Stay in this place for a while, allowing your body and mind to imaginatively occupy this space for a moment.
- After you've soaked in all the sensory details of the space, flex your fingers, wiggle your toes, and rotate your shoulders. Drop your chin to your chest and swing your head back and forth. Blink your eyes open.
- Have participants immediately start writing what comes to their minds, letting the descriptive details flow in a stream of consciousness. They can capture their story by drawing.

The guided imagery and deep breathing stimulates creative pathways in the brain and quiets the regions of logical and critical thinking. It's always amazing to watch participants dive into a creative task with the focus and intense energy that this exercise unleashes—we find it hard to cut them off when the time is up. They reflect with awe on how the experience releases creative energy. Sometimes participants are surprised to discover that they have poetry and vivid language inside themselves.

One participant shared the language she crafted during a guided-imagery session at the 2014 Creative Problem Solving Institute. Even though English is a second language for Sumara Regina Ancona Lopes, this exercise unleashed poetic phrases that took her to the beaches and mountains of her Brazilian homeland: "The water moves in ripples as if dancing in the soft wind. The leaves on the trees sway back and forth, back and forth, cutting the silence of the old mountains, singing a song of love to the birds flying around."

Storyboarding

This exercise involves engaging stakeholders in the process of mapping out a story that starts with the current circumstances and progresses to a desired future state in which the proposed vision has been achieved. Teams can work individually or as a group to visualize the plot points through pictures and phrases. They might use clippings from magazines, images from the internet, or simple drawings to illustrate their ideas. We like to have individual participants fill in the story elements from their point of view and share their ideas in small groups.

The example shows how a team might use a storyboard to develop an influencer communication plan to promote the benefits of dairy to athletes. The team starts with a challenge statement, then connects the current state to a desired future state through visuals and text that define the key milestones.

Storyboard Example

Challenge: How might we influence sports professionals to promote the benefits of dairy to athletes?

Current State

Athletes, coaches, and trainers turn to supplements rather than food

Scientific controversy

↓

Need proof

Doctors and sports dietitians explain science to coaches and trainers

"If coach says it works, it must be true."

Winning teams refuel with dairy

Future State

Everyday athletes refuel with milk, yogurt, and dairy beverages

A word to the wise: junior and cross-functional team members sometimes won't have the perspective or skills to imagine the future state. In these cases, it's better to work with the leader or a leadership team ahead of the session to identify the current and future states. Then have the group fill in the story elements that plot a path to the future state.

Possible Variation

Find photos that serve as metaphors and combine them with storyboarding. Provide each team with a set of random images from a photo deck. Ask them to assign one image to each storyboard box to help stimulate their thinking about that part of the story.

Story Prompts

During visioning exercises, it can be helpful to offer story prompts that help participants generate their story ideas. For example, when developing story prompts related to a vision about a new product or system that is being rolled out in a company, you might build off a stem such as, "Imagine your work life five years from now." Then encourage participants to ponder specifics of the proposed future, and invite them to write and draw stories that reflect what they imagine. Here are some prompts that might be useful:

- What if you were voted Employee of the Year? Craft a story to describe what you did and how you earned the honor.
- What does "a day in the life" of your job look like?
- Who do you encounter?
- What tensions or struggles will you need to overcome?
- How might your work be more rewarding?
- What life lessons or leadership values might help you function in this new reality?

In addition to the story-crafting tools introduced in this chapter, many others are sprinkled throughout this book. Consider pairing the tools introduced in later chapters with the story prompts above to support the visioning process.

Closing Thoughts

Many visionary leaders have a knack for using stories to help others imagine and get excited about possibilities. Often they're gifted storytellers who are living their own remarkable narrative that might involve experiences of isolation and derision for being a little—or certifiably—crazy. Innovation leaders can learn from these visionaries about how to create a bold vision and get others excited about it. Becoming a visionary leader requires imagination and a deep understanding of the opportunity, along with the ability to connect dots and persuade others. Stories do all of that and more.

As the parable about the blind men and the elephant illustrates, when we only touch one part of a whole, we misunderstand what's actually there. A well-crafted story can help the blind men see.

This chapter explores how stories help leaders forge a vision and engage team members to feel they're part of it. When others invest in your vision as their own, they're inspired to make it become reality.

For additional resources on stories and visioning, you may wish to explore the body of literature on appreciative inquiry, the *dream* phase in particular. Those who work with appreciative inquiry have created useful resources about how to build a vision from a collective set of stories stimulated by a story prompt about a "best" experience.

The only thing worse than being blind is having sight and no vision.

—Helen Keller

3

Exploring and Clarifying with Stories

How stories can deepen insights and build empathy

"Pat Was in a Panic"

By Jean Storlie

Early in my career as a dietitian/fitness specialist, I answered a panicky phone call from a participant in my weight-loss program. Pat (not her real name) said, "Jean, I have a problem. I really need to talk to you." She'd been a "perfect" participant: she never missed class, her food diaries and exercise log showed stellar compliance, and her weight loss was steady. After three months, Pat was walking five miles a day and had lost fifteen pounds and 5 percent of her body fat. When she graduated from the program, she was feeling confident about her new lifestyle. So I was really excited to hear from her.

With a shaky voice, Pat told me that when getting out of bed that morning, she looked down and saw "skinny legs." I applauded her hard work and results—but that only increased her agitation. I listened as Pat continued, "I went downstairs, reached into the cupboard, and saw a skinny arm." Perplexed, I responded, "I'm sorry, Pat, but I don't see the problem." She blurted, "Jean you don't understand. I'm starting to believe that I can be a thin person. What am I going to do? People might want to talk to me at parties—what am I going to say? I'm just Jim's wife. No one talks to me. Maybe I need to go to college or get a job . . . I don't know what to do."

I ran into Pat on campus a few years later. She'd enrolled in college and divorced Jim but, unfortunately, had regained her lost weight. She was happy and excited about her future. Her life was crazy as a single mom who was working and going to school. She hoped to get back to a regular exercise routine when her life settled down because, she said, "I felt so great when I was walking five miles a day!"

When Success Is as Defeating as Failure

Pat taught Jean that the fear of success can be as debilitating as the fear of failure when people struggle with their weight and self-image. Jean also learned that scientific facts and motivational gimmicks don't help clients change until they address deeper issues. After Pat's call, Jean started to tune in to her clients' stories and create forums for participants to share their stories. The story-sharing sessions inspired more engagement and compliance than fact-based nutrition education classes. Participants explored the challenges and successes of life changes in the context of their wellness goals. The sessions also fostered connections among participants who supported and mentored each other through change.

Sharing stories and giving witness to other people's stories can transform people's lives. WW (formerly Weight Watchers), which has over a million active members worldwide, has built a multinational business around sharing stories of success. Many pyramid sales organizations successfully leverage viral storytelling. They tap into the power of the narrative trope "I succeeded; you can too." When companies and health care providers approach weight management simply as a calories-in and calories-out equation, they miss the true picture of what weight strugglers experience.

This chapter explores how stories can help teams explore and clarify creative challenges. Stories uncover deeper meanings by bringing empathy and different perspectives into focus, and they put data into context. *Story listening* sits at the center of exploration and the clarification of creative challenges. Innovators gain clarity about an opportunity and its underlying challenges when they give witness to the constellation of stories related to the situation. As Ursula K. Le Guin said, "There are no right answers to wrong questions." In this chapter, you'll discover how stories can help you find the right questions.

Stories Uncover Deeper Meanings

Most innovation and change initiatives involve an exploratory, discovery, immersion phase to gather data and insights that help clarify the problem at hand. In the creative problem solving (CPS) model, this stage is called *clarify*.

Often teams compile large volumes of data and analytics but fall short in synthesizing the information in a way that conveys the nuances and complexities associated with the problem. Stories can illuminate what's going on beneath the surface and help a team explore deeper meanings and make sense of the data. Let's go back to Pat's story, which reveals deep, dark emotions that many dieters experience but marketers and innovators may not understand. Demographic and lifestyle data fail to reveal Pat's weight-loss struggles and the other life issues she's faced. Even psychological theory and terminology can't fully convey her pain and agony. By combining data and analytics with stories, business teams become more sensitive to their users' underlying emotions, which will help them develop more effective marketing messages, product ideas, and engagement strategies.

Trigger Empathy

The brain releases oxytocin—a hormone that produces feelings of empathy, compassion, and trust—in response to a good narrative. That biological response helps explain why stories can be such a powerful way to create the kind of goodwill with others that can lead to innovation and other business goals.

Chances are your consumers and users have personal narratives that involve people, conflict, and change— the headline elements of a good story. Curating their stories might be relevant to solving an innovation, branding, technical, or marketing challenge. By listening to consumers' and users' stories, you can learn what's working and what's not in the current state. In our innovation work, we use stories and story-listening tools to help our clients gain empathy for the users who will benefit from a new solution.

If you're in a position to participate in consumer or user research, listen for their stories to gain empathy for how they experience your product. In chapter 5 we explore the Design Thinking model, in which empathy is the first step in the process. Ethnographic research and observation helps a team gain empathy for users.

Stories from the people who influence and surround users can also illuminate struggles and emotions that users experience. For example, Jean has shared stories from her decade of experience in leading weight loss programs with a number of food and wellness innovation teams to help them design products and services for weight-conscious consumers. One innovation team coupled Jean's stories with in-depth ethnographic work, which reinforced and elaborated on insights from stories like Pat's. Through these stories and observations, the business team began to witness and internalize the painful and defeating feelings that dieters often experience. Some of their product and message ideas addressed deeper emotional needs, such as the fear of failure (and success), anger, and victimization. The opportunity maps the team created included more emotional context and unique ways to connect with consumers who struggle with weight loss.

Becoming skilled at retelling user stories that are gathered during fieldwork can help an innovation team relay what they witness firsthand to senior leaders and execution teams. In retelling these stories, innovators help others gain empathy for users. Chapter 5 discusses tools and techniques for capturing and telling user stories.

Ethnography

Ethnography is a qualitative research method that involves hands-on, on-the-scene learning. It's a primary research method for social and cultural anthropology and has grown in popularity in the consumer insights field over the last decade. Ethnographic studies require the researcher to immerse themselves in the everyday life of the subjects they study. Ethnographers interact with and observe consumers in their homes and other places that comprise their day-to-day life. They might accompany consumers on shopping trips or go with them to the gym or a favorite restaurant.

Ethnographers rely on observation as the primary data collection method. Field notes are written with details about what a person says and does, how he or she interacts with others, as well as the language, rituals, and symbols that populate the person's life. What is not said is as important as what is said.

Put Data into Context

Annette Simmons asserts, "Stories give facts meaning. Facts give stories substance." Clarifying involves digging into data to extract meaning. Facts and data are critical to understanding a problem, but they don't reveal all the issues and opportunities. When data is combined with stories, a fuller picture of the consumer's struggles emerges, allowing a team to understand its users at a more visceral level. By shedding new light on situations, stories help connect the dots between different data points and make sense of statistics. Facts answer the *what*. Stories help you see the *so what?*

Teams generally gather scientific and technical information, market research, competitor comparisons, and consumer data when they immerse themselves in an opportunity. During immersion sessions, strategically placed stories can enhance the communication of this technical information to cross-functional team members.

Story tools are particularly helpful in extracting the deeper meaning from consumer research, which can be packaged in a spectrum of ways. Insights researchers might get intrigued with raw data and summary reports, but they aren't very helpful to other team members. Often, insights professionals synthesize the research to create a consumer profile that includes data and some insights. Some go a little further and develop consumer personas that portray the consumer as a character with a name, face, and personality traits. They might include a day-in-the-life illustration or tell a story about the character, but generally personas focus more on describing the characteristics and traits of a target group. Consumer narratives go further, sharing the consumer's struggle and journey. They help innovation teams and stakeholders experience more empathy and understanding for the consumer.

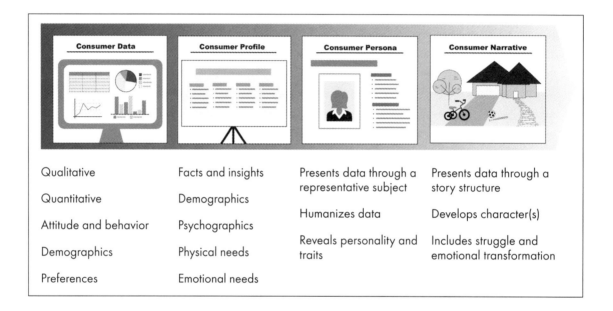

Consumer Data	Consumer Profile	Consumer Persona	Consumer Narrative
Qualitative	Facts and insights	Presents data through a representative subject	Presents data through a story structure
Quantitative	Demographics	Humanizes data	Develops character(s)
Attitude and behavior	Psychographics	Reveals personality and traits	Includes struggle and emotional transformation
Demographics	Physical needs		
Preferences	Emotional needs		

Compare and Contrast a Consumer Profile, Persona, and Narrative

Read the consumer demographics and profile, and then answer the questions. Do the same with the consumer persona and consumer narrative.

Consumer Demographics

Boomers cover a wide age range, so grouping them into one cohort does not recognize the various life stages that they might be experiencing. Demographers often break them into two cohorts: Older Boomers (born 1948–55) and Younger Boomers (born 1956–63).

Older Boomers (born 1948–55)	Younger Boomers (born 1956–63)
May still be working or in a second career	Might still be working
Pursuing travel and other leisure activities	Thinking about retirement
Might be grandparents	May still be supporting kids who live at home
Health changes may be affecting life priorities	Showing signs of aging (change in sleep patterns, joint pain, vision deterioration, weight gain)
Parents have passed or need help	Possibly caring for ailing parents

Consumer Profile

Although Boomers find themselves dealing with the health effects of aging, they are approaching this life stage with the same optimism and defiance that defined their coming-of-age era.

Top Health Concerns	Key Insights
Healthy weight	Exhibit optimism and defiance
Energy	Defy traditional views of aging
Mobility	Have lost parents or friends to disease
Digestive health	Know they're not invincible, but hope to beat odds through healthy living
Heart health	Seek solutions inside and outside traditional medicine

Questions

- What key insights do you glean from the data?
- Do you see any story elements in the data?
- What type of a story might you create from this information?
- Did you gain any empathy for this consumer?

Consumer Persona

I'm Gloria, a sixty-one-year-old lawyer, wife, and mother of three grown children. I believe in living an active lifestyle and eating healthy so I can fight the effects of aging. I want to run around and play with my grandchildren rather than sit in a chair and watch them.

Consumer Narrative

I'm Gloria, a sixty-one-year-old lawyer, wife, and mother of three grown children. When I was twenty-eight, my dad died from a sudden heart attack. Sensitive and charming, he was always there for me. Twenty-five years later, I still miss him. It was traumatic to lose him at such a young age, but his passing made me realize the hazards of unhealthy habits. He smoked heavily and was overweight and sedentary. Because of this experience, living healthy has been a core value for me and my family. We eat well and stay active.

Ten years ago, I was shocked to learn that I have fibromyalgia, which causes low-level chronic pain and debilitating flare-ups. Shortly after that, my husband was diagnosed with hypertension. It pulled me back to those dark days after my dad died. But we doubled down on our commitment to health—neither of us want to end up in a nursing home on twenty medications—and discovered new ways to live healthy. We practice yoga and eat more fresh, local foods. We took a cooking class and found a fun new hobby that has brought more joy to our food preparations.

Despite all our efforts to live healthy and stay off meds, we still experience signs of aging, like needing reading glasses, sleep disturbances, and joint stiffness.

Questions

- Does the narrative reflect the consumer data?
- Did you gain empathy for this consumer target because of the narrative?
- Does the narrative representation of the data affect how you internalized the consumer insights?
- How might you use stories to explore consumer insights?

Reveal Different Perspectives

Like a kaleidoscope, stories shift perspective to reveal new patterns and possibilities. When solving business problems, it's useful to extract stories from people close to the issues. For example, in designing products for the weight-management consumer, a team might engage with dietitians, physicians, weight-loss counselors, and coaches to understand their perspectives. Their stories and viewpoints illuminate compelling facets of a problem or clarify other stories, data, and insights. By collecting stories from users, influencers, and stakeholders, you can gather a comprehensive perspective on the situation. For a deeper understanding, explore their hopes and dreams as well as their pain points about the challenge.

As you uncover different points of view about a business situation—from consumers, customers, employees, executives, competitors, and thought leaders—their perspectives will illuminate both subtle and distinct viewpoints on the same situation. Sometimes alternative perspectives contribute new color commentary to the same story; other times they reveal an entirely new meaning. When different perspectives of the same situation converge on the same experience, you've found a universal insight. When they vary widely, you've stumbled onto a tension or potential roadblock. These stories individually and collectively reveal the larger landscape that surrounds a challenge

Consider who, inside and outside the organization, can offer alternative perspectives on the challenge. Capture the themes that emerge and apply these insights to the problem at hand. To open a team to alternative perspectives, try The Cookie Thief exercise to inspire a productive conversation about how an incorrect perception can lead to false assumptions.

Exercise: Change Perspectives and Disrupt Assumptions

Read "The Cookie Thief" aloud in unison. Alternatively, select a group of volunteers to read segments of the story in succession (with feeling!). You could also have everyone read silently, but the first two approaches have the advantage of unifying the group in a shared experience.

"The Cookie Thief" by Valerie Cox

A woman was waiting at an airport one night, with several long hours before her flight. She hunted for a book in the airport shops, bought a bag of cookies and found a place to drop.

She was engrossed in her book but happened to see that the man sitting beside her was as bold as could be. He grabbed a cookie or two from the bag sitting between them, which she tried to ignore to avoid a scene.

So she munched the cookies and watched the clock as the gutsy cookie thief diminished her stock. She was getting more irritated as the minutes ticked by, thinking, "If I wasn't so nice, I would blacken his eye."

With each cookie she took, he took one too. When only one was left, she wondered what he would do. With a smile on his face, and a nervous laugh, he took the last cookie and broke it in half.

He offered her half as he ate the other—she snatched it from him and thought. Oooh, brother ... This guy has some nerve, and he's also rude. Why he didn't even show any gratitude!

She had never known when she had been so galled and sighed with relief when her flight was called. She gathered her belongings and headed to the gate, refusing to look back at the thieving ingrate.

She boarded the plane and sank in her seat, then she sought her book, which was almost complete. As she reached in her baggage, she gasped with surprise: her bag of cookies was in front of her eyes.

"If mine are here," she moaned in despair, "the others were his, and he tried to share." Too late to apologize, she realized with grief that she was the rude one, the ingrate, the thief.

Debrief the Story
- What were you thinking as you listened to the story unfold?
- What makes this a good story?
- What does the story teach us?

Optional Exercise
Have participants grab a partner, and share a time when they jumped to conclusions too quickly or gave someone the benefit of the doubt. Give participants time to discuss what happened as a result, share stories, and exchange ideas.

Story Listening Unlocks Insights

Story listening is a critical skill for innovation leaders. Stories and story fragments naturally surface during immersion activities and provide a glimpse into the emotions that color the landscape of the challenge. Become more attuned to stories that tumble out organically. In addition, sharpen your skills in eliciting stories through stakeholder interviews, focus groups, ethnography, and team working sessions. User stories are pivotal, but you will get a more complete picture if you also capture stories shared by employees, stakeholders, and competitors.

Clarifying through Listening

A story-oriented approach to the clarification and exploration of creative challenges fosters teamwork, continuous learning, and conflict resolution. Stories illuminate insights on intangible, difficult-to-evaluate projects. Story-based research with users delves deeper into emotional insights and can be used to overcome the limitations of traditional research (e.g., interviews and surveys) with internal teams, clients, or consumers. Chapter 5 includes additional tips on how to capture and retell user stories.

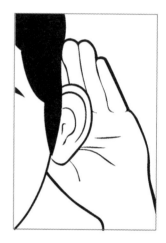

Story Listening Techniques

Disengage from digital devices to listen attentively and capture the key narrative elements. Your undivided attention engenders trust. Seek stories through prompts related to the challenge to be solved. Once stories start to flow, listen with delight and undivided attention to extract more meaning and insight from what these contributors have to share. For more specific guidance, refer to appendix C, which provides a primer on how to craft interview questions to elicit stories.

As you listen, make note of the elements of the story (e.g., setting, characters, and plot points) so you can retell it later. Ask follow-up questions to fill in any important missing elements.

Story Techniques for Exploration and Clarification

Stories from end users, influencers, and stakeholders woven together with facts create a big-picture view of the issue. Also, personal, professional, corporate, and brand stories might be used to help a team process data and extract meaningful insights. Stories along with data help to clarify a problem and explore it from different points of view.

Empathy Mapping of User Groups

One exercise to process insights from users is to populate an empathy map with data from consumer research. Creating the map helps a team create insights about the data they gathered, then internalize it through an emotional context. Empathy maps also serve as a springboard for crafting stories. Users' traits and characteristics can lead to possible storylines as members of the team imagine different episodes that people like this might experience.

Team members can work individually, in pairs, or in small groups to create and share a variety of stories. These stories help the team make sense of the research and internalize emotionally oriented insights.

Consumer or User Stories

Story-based techniques for gathering and communicating consumer and user research help the team and key stakeholders build empathy and intuition for the challenges these people face. Using story-crafting techniques, consumer research teams can present their findings in ways that emotionally resonate with their audiences.

Think and Feel
What does this person think and feel?

Hear
What does this person hear?

See
What does this person see?

Say and Do
What does this person say and do?

Gain
What solves their problems?

Pain
What causes them problems or pain?

Source: *Gamestorming: A Playbook for Innovators, Rulebreakers, and Changemakers* (O'Reilly Media, 2010). Used with permission.

Enhance qualitative and ethnographic research by prompting the people who use the product or service to tell stories, then listen carefully and make note of vivid details that reveal the plot (i.e., conflict or tension, moment of truth, and emotional transformation). Enhance discussion guides with cues and prompts to elicit narrative elements and details so you can construct powerful narratives on the back end. Over time, you'll get more attuned to recognizing and giving witness to rich stories that reveal pivotal insights about users. Refer to chapter 5 for more guidance on how to gather user stories, including specific tools and techniques to prompt users to share stories and methods to capture those stories. Chapter 5 also delves into considerations for crafting user stories, such as selecting the voice (i.e., perspective), and tips for oral storytelling, writing stories, and using clips from user interactions.

Once user stories are gathered, look for themes and common elements among them. We often see that their stories reflect universal plots, or *archetypes*. David Hutchens's *Circle of the 9 Muses* sixteen universal plots illustrate a wide range of human experiences in a graphic and understandable format.

Another tool that we use when interpreting user stories is Carol Pearson's Narrative Intelligence counseling model, based on twelve archetypes that form the basis of a psychometric test, the Pearson-Marr Archetype Indicator (PMAI®). Her work has its roots in counseling psychology, in which facilitators help their patients heal through understanding the narratives they've been living. She envisions archetypes as inner allies that express a person's capacities and fears. As Pearson's approach gained notoriety, it's been applied to leadership, insights, and innovation.

We use Hutchens's universal plots and Pearson's Narrative Intelligence archetypes to synthesize and make sense of user stories. For example, let's plot out Pat's story in the context of Hutchens's Journey to the Heart archetype to illustrate how Jean's experience with Pat changed her approach to nutrition and weight-loss counseling. When sharing and processing user stories during the clarification stage, explore how these plots and archetypes can help you understand users' stories in the context of universal human experiences. If you see a connection between a user story and a universal plot, you've probably tapped into a powerful insight.

Journey to the Heart

Business as usual was disrupted by situation that demanded a more human response	Responded with vulnerability, love, compassion, or kindness	Someone's life was changed	Everyone was touched or changed	Today we invite human considerations into our work

Pat's Story Changed Jean's Work

Pat presented a deeper struggle	Jean listened and gave witness to her story	Jean realized there are deeper challenges in weight loss	Jean adopted a more empathetic approach	Jean found the power of stories

Connecting Pat's Story to a Universal Plot. Inspired by the graphics that appear in *Circle of the Nine Muses* by David Hutchens. Used with permission.

Campfire Story Circles

Campfires ignite story sharing. Someone tells a tale and before you know it, stories ping-pong around the fire. This activity creates the mood and environment of a campfire—relaxed, warm, comfortable, trusting, and organic—where participants feel free to share stories and give witness to other people's stories. Simulating a campfire circle is a quick and easy way to collect stories from groups of people (project teams, stakeholders, consumers, end users, etc.).

During discovery and clarification, campfire story circles can help a team extract meaning out of the data they've gathered. By sharing stories along with data and analytics, the team gains empathy, clarifies insights, and understands the *why*. Team members can share stories they observed in ethnographic work with users or stories about their own experiences with the product or service (or an analogous product or service). For example, if a doctor's office or wellness program wants to improve its quality of care, a campfire story circle could focus on sharing the best and worst health-care experiences members of the team have experienced. This approach can also be used in sessions with consumers and users to gather stories about their unmet needs and how they use a product or service.

Download a campfire app onto a mobile device (numerous options include images of flickering flames accompanied by the crackling sounds of a fire burning). Set up a circle of chairs or seat everyone around a table. Dim the lights to create the atmosphere of a campfire. Put the "burning fire" in the middle of the circle and use story prompts related to the project and key insights to get the stories started. If it's important to capture the stories accurately, use an audio recording rather than notetaking to keep the conversation flowing naturally. We like to ask each group to identify the best story (based on whatever criteria they decide) from their discussion and the insight it illustrates before they rejoin the large group discussion.

Shawn Callahan, author of *Putting Stories to Work* and founder of the Australian firm Anecdote, promotes "anecdote circles," which have gained popularity in the business storytelling and insights communities. The concept is very similar to campfire story circles, focusing on brief accounts of an incident or event that have an interesting or amusing twist. Both stories and anecdotes will tumble out in campfire story circles.

Guided Imagery

Guided imagery was introduced in chapter 2 as a way to explore a vision, but it can also be used to examine key assumptions as you explore and clarify. Using the same method, guided imagery plus a story can help a team process facts and data with empathy. User, influencer, employee, and founder stories in combination with a guided-imagery journey reveal a multitude of perspectives that deepen insights and nurture creative collaboration.

Use guided imagery to take stakeholders or team members on a "mini-vacation" into another point of view. Invite them to explore different perspectives of the situation. Breathing exercises along with verbal cues transport participants into a relaxed state where imagination flows. By sharing a relevant story during guided imagery, the story is experienced vividly—and viscerally.

This activity works best when participants are provided a cushion of three to five minutes to reflect privately and capture their thoughts before they debrief with others. It's helpful to ease them into larger group dialogue by first having them share in pairs or triplets. Then Snowball Pair and Share can help build a shared narrative.

Readings

Rather than asking participants to read a research report before coming to an innovation work session, consider having them read a story that takes three to five minutes but leaves them reflecting on deeper truths. You can also forgo the pre-read and bring the reading into the workshop. Fables, children's books, ballads, and real-life tales are easy ways to bring a story into a clarification session. You might also share a video or written story about a user. Just make sure that you select a story that triggers a deeper emotion or meaning and leaves them pondering the challenge from a more holistic perspective.

Appreciative Inquiry

Appreciative inquiry (AI) was introduced in chapter 2 for its potential to rally stakeholders and constituents around a shared vision. But stories collected during the AI process can also help teams extract meaning and purpose from data collected during discovery and clarification. The first two stages of AI—discover and dream—use story-based techniques that can help focus energy on what motivates constituents. The best-of stories from the discover stage feed into the dream stage, where the most meaningful stories illuminate the path (or paths) forward. Stories provide both the grist and the filter for finding meaningful solutions.

Closing Thoughts

We've both worked on business teams comprised of people who can be blinded by their bias for action. They see a problem, quickly select a solution, and start executing a plan. Weeks or months later, the project starts to swirl and derail. Someone says, "Maybe we need to back up and approach this differently." Time and resources were wasted because the team chased a solution that failed to address the root cause of a problem.

Unfortunately, many teams feel pressed for time. They assume the clarification of a challenge takes too long, so they skip or skim over this step. They pursue solutions that address the problem area but not the core issue, which results in wasted time. Bias for action is good, but it needs to be tempered with exploration and clarification. On the flip side, rewinding endlessly in the discovery stage without progressing into action is equally dysfunctional. Gifted leaders have the wisdom and intuition to balance when to clarify and when to move forward with action.

Pat's story reveals that users' stories, as well as stories from others who interact with users, bring hidden insights to the surface. Coupled with data and analytics, stories paint a broad picture that helps a team gain empathy for the users and clarify the problem to solve.

This chapter addresses the importance of listening for stories that organically surface during the exploration and clarification stage, as well as prompting people to tell stories. (Appendix C delves deeper into interview techniques to elicit stories.) We also expand on how the concept of archetypes and universal plots can help teams interpret and make sense of the stories they gather during discovery. Empathy mapping, campfire story circles, guided imagery, and AI are other story-based tools that help during exploration and clarification.

If I had an hour to solve a problem, I'd spend fifty-five minutes defining it and five minutes solving it.
—ALBERT EINSTEIN

4

Storytelling in Ideation

How storytelling can spark the flow of ideas

"The Intern Was Right"
By Mimi Sherlock

As we strolled across the building and descended the stairs, I chatted with Suzie, an undergraduate intern, about the company's change initiative, the topic of the meeting we were about to attend. I thought exposing her to a meeting with senior leaders would be a treat for her—and this was a plum project for me. I expounded on the value of candor and feedback, coaching her to observe the team dynamics and be prepared to share her observations.

The quiet, subdued area occupied by HR on the lower level lacked the vibrant energy of the main floors. We joined several department heads who had gathered around a large conference table in a beige room. Heads nodded as Lydia, the HR director, a professionally coifed, well-mannered woman, outlined the executive team's plans to roll out a culture-change project intended to transform employee engagement. In the last ten minutes of the meeting, Lydia expressed concern about employee backlash and asked for ideas about how to successfully execute the change.

Living up to my reputation as a prolific ideator, I quickly spouted fourteen ideas. Thinking I'd offered valuable contributions to the meeting—and modeled "thinking on my feet" for Suzie—I was surprised when no one responded. Lydia nodded politely, glanced at her watch, and gathered her papers. She looked up with a stiff smile and graciously thanked everyone for coming. The group dispersed, politely chitchatting as they filed out of the room.

Back in my office, I asked Suzie what she thought about the meeting. This twenty-two-year-old undergrad looked me in the eye and told me I'd overwhelmed Lydia and disrupted the meeting. It's a good thing I was sitting down . . . The world started to spin around me. I was aghast at her audacity . . . humiliated . . . outraged.

Then with a sinking feeling, I knew Suzie was right. I realized that my talent for ideation—which had always contributed to my success—isn't always helpful or appropriate.

Why My Fourteen Ideas Fell Flat

That unexpected feedback occurred more than twenty years ago, yet Mimi thinks about it frequently. She went into the meeting believing the axioms "it takes a lot of ideas to come up with a good one" and "the first idea isn't always the best." She'd been trained in Osborn-Parnes Creative Problem Solving, which espouses these principles. Mimi still believes in them, but since that experience, she constantly assesses the people and situation before turning on the spigot of ideas that naturally flow from her extroverted brain.

Mimi also learned that sometimes we shouldn't take people literally: when Lydia asked for ideas, she was actually seeking solutions. Ten minutes before the end of a meeting isn't the time to spark a round of ideation (the common term for brainstorming activities structured to generate new ideas and concepts). Generating a plethora of raw ideas is a first step, but it's not sufficient. Even though ideation is often depicted as a freewheeling, uninhibited process that endorses wacky ideas, a successful ideation requires both divergent and convergent thinking. Only after sifting through raw ideas to deliberately select the best ones will you discover viable solutions.

This chapter explores ways to use stories and story techniques in both the divergent and convergent facets of ideation. We'll also examine research that links storytelling to ideation and creativity, and we'll share practical tips on how to bring the magic of stories into ideation sessions.

Stories Spark the Flow of Ideas

Like magic, stories connect the synapses between logic and emotion, unlocking pathways to creative thinking. They transport us to a more imaginative state—the perfect mind space for ideation. After experiencing a story, teams are more able to generate ideas that stretch beyond the obvious and touch on emotional insights.

Ideation is the second stage of the CPS model. It relies on brainstorming activities to generate a wide range of ideas and solutions before selecting the options with the highest potential for solving the problem. Stories in combination with ideation tools help a team get into a freewheeling mind-set where ideas flow. Because stories tug on heartstrings, they also stimulate ideas that have more empathy and emotional context.

Neuroscience on Relaxation and Playfulness

Stories help people relax, suspend belief, and enter a more playful state—all of which support creative thinking. Brain imaging studies show that relaxation and playfulness stimulate areas of the brain associated with creativity. Higher levels of dopamine (a hormone associated with euphoria) improve creativity. People are more creative when they're in a positive mood. Relaxing activities like meditating, exercising, or showering can increase creativity. They provide an opportunity to step back and get a fresh perspective on a gnarly problem or flawed solution.

On the flip side, stress and uncertainty lead to conventional choices, causing us to overlook creative solutions and avoid taking risks. During stress, the amygdala (the region of the brain responsible for emotions, emotional behavior, and motivation) shuts down the cerebral cortex (both hemispheres) and prepares us for fight or flight.

Neuroscience research related to play shows that adults are more likely to engage in learning when they're in a positive emotional state—in other words, when they're having fun. Playfulness makes intimidating tasks shrink and perplexing material easier to digest and comprehend. When in a "state of play," people are more likely to explore what's possible. Research about neuroscience and play reveals the following:

- Play increases imagination
- Play creates a simultaneous sense of safety and adventure
- Play invokes creativity
- Play encourages us to adapt to the outside world while remaining authentic

Flow

Have you ever experienced a time when, suddenly, all the pieces click together and you lose yourself in time? Hours might melt away while you solve a problem that seemed unsolvable or you create something that was unimaginable before. You might forget to eat or miss an appointment. In his influential 1975 book *Flow: The Psychology of Optimal Experience*, Mihály Csíkszentmihályi named this experience flow—complete absorption in a productive activity, such that you lose touch with space and time.

When people experience flow, they feel like something magical has happened. Stories help team members fully immerse in a situation, which can ease them into a state of flow. Simply put, stories make it easy to immerse, immersion gets the flow going, and flow sparks ideas and creative thinking.

More Background on Flow

Sometimes called being "in the zone," Csíkszentmihályi describes flow as the mental state in which a person performing an activity is fully immersed in a feeling of energized focus, full involvement, and enjoyment in the process of the activity.

He questions the belief that gifted artists were touched by a muse "like a bolt of lightning," which stemmed from Greek and Roman mythology. Countering this mystic belief, Csíkszentmihályi argues that flow is achieved by "filling up" or immersing in the creative challenge. For example, a writer isn't blocked because the lightning bolt hasn't struck, but perhaps because he or she hasn't sufficiently immersed in the topic and more research is needed.

Csíkszentmihályi also advocates that stepping away from a nagging problem can help to solve it. Engaging in playful, recreational, and relaxing activities often trigger flow.

Creative Styles and Ideation

As an Ideator, Mimi often dazzles others with her innate ability to imagine possibilities and quickly generate ideas. But as her intern so wisely pointed out, Ideators sometimes overwhelm others with their flood of ideas if they have no self-awareness. People with a range of styles bring complementary energies to the innovation process. Facilitators who lead ideation sessions can benefit from understanding the different ways individuals contribute to innovation and tailor each session accordingly.

Two assessments, the FourSight® Thinking Profile and the Team Dimensions Profile, provide insights into how people contribute to innovation and collaborative work. The FourSight Thinking Profile is based on Osborn-Parnes' CPS model. The Team Dimensions Profile is similar, but it carves out an additional role for people who recognize great ideas and "sell them" to others. Appendix D provides additional background about the FourSight and Team Dimensions Profile creative styles assessments.

FourSight Thinking Profile

In the early 1990s, Gerard Puccio, PhD, a professor of creative studies at Buffalo State, part of the State University of New York, began to investigate the correlation between individual behavior and creative problem solving. After a decade of rigorous testing and validation, he put his theory into practice through the FourSight Thinking Profile. The tool measures individuals' preferences for different components of the innovation process and offers meaningful insights on how people contribute differently to problem solving.

The profile categorizes people into four archetypal roles for creative problem solving:

- Clarifier
- Ideator
- Developer
- Implementer

The profile also recognizes that some people have combinations of preferences. All told, there are fifteen possible profiles, with some preferring one style and others landing in a two- or three-way preference. One profile, the Integrator, reflects an even balance among all four thinking styles.

Every style, including the Integrator, has its Herculean strengths and its Achilles' heel, but collaborating with people who have other styles can shore up these pitfalls. That said, when those with diverse skills, perspectives, and blind spots work together, their differences can produce conflict. Managing team dynamics to optimize everyone's strengths is a key part of creative collaboration.

Team Dimensions Profile

Observation and research by Allen N. Fahden and Srinivasan Namakkal over two decades identified distinct approaches to thought and behavior when people collaborate. This led them to theorize that people's natural thinking and behavioral preferences influence the roles they play in a team. Fahden and Namakkal developed an assessment inventory that was tested and validated by Wiley and published as the Team Dimensions Profile. It is currently available through the Everything DiSC® Authorized Partner network. The model is constructed on a two-dimensional matrix that characterizes how people approach their work: conceptual, spontaneous, normative, and methodical.

An individual's score on these continua indicates the roles they prefer to play on a team. Many people blend two roles. Some people move fluidly across all four; they're called the *Flexers*. Refer to appendix D for more information on the Team Dimensions Profile. A key concept in this model is that high-performing teams have people from all four quadrants, and they smoothly pass tasks back and forth to each other. The Z shape at the center of the model represents the way batons pass in high-performing teams.

Myers-Briggs Type Indicator

The Myers-Briggs Type Indicator® (MBTI) is the most widely known instrument for understanding personality differences. It's based on Carl Jung's theory of psychological type (i.e., normal differences in people's behavior result from inborn tendencies to use their minds differently). These innate preferences are depicted through four continua that yield sixteen types or preferences:

- Extroversion–Introversion
- Sensing–Intuition
- Thinking–Feeling
- Judging–Perceiving

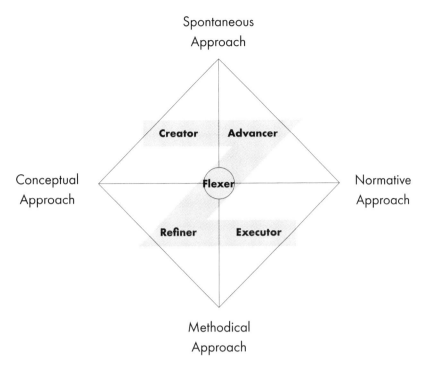

Team Dimensions Profile figure: © 2005 by John Wiley & Sons, Inc. All rights reserved. Reprinted with permission from John Wiley & Sons, Inc.

Sharing Our Styles

Jean initially scored as an Ideator with FourSight, but she found that she was a fish out of water when placed in a group of Ideators. "They were popping out ideas like popcorn, while I stood pondering the problem. I felt so overwhelmed," Jean recalls. "When they all commiserated about how hard it is to follow through, I knew I was in the wrong group." Upon further examination, Jean realized she's an Integrator. With the Team Dimensions Profile, she scores as a Creator-Refiner with some Advancer tendencies. On the MBTI, she's an ENTP (Extroverted, Intuitive, Thinking, and Perceptive). Though energized when executing a new idea, day-to-day operations drain her energy.

As revealed by Mimi's "The Intern Was Right" story, she is a FourSight Ideator through and through. She describes herself as a style-assessment junkie. On the Team Dimensions Profile, Mimi is a Creator trending toward an Advancer. Like Jean, she is a Myers-Briggs ENTP. Although she is a prolific Ideator, Mimi believes that the NT (Intuitive and Thinking) part of her MBTI signals her competence to produce buttoned-up ideas. She loves to clarify and develop, but she's wiped out when it's time to implement. She yearns for another creative task. Despite having a thinking preference, her capacity for empathy is strong and dominant.

In this book's opening story, we describe how we immediately experienced a mind meld that was intensely creative and productive. Our compatibility can be partially explained through both the similarities and differences in our creative styles. As ENTPs, we both start by looking at the big picture. We see patterns and possibilities where others see chaos. And we support our ideas with facts and analysis. Mimi's proclivity for ideation jump-starts our thinking, and Jean's skills as a FourSight Integrator help us clarify the problem and advance our ideas through the execution phase. The Team Dimensions Profile further highlights our compatibility. We both score with dominant Creator tendencies, with Jean also showing strength as a Refiner and Mimi leaning into the Advancer mode. Neither of us love implementation, but Jean can get energized by turning a new idea into a reality. As with any fruitful collaboration, our success lies in the way our similarities and differences harmonize.

Stories Enable Innovation Across All Styles

Regardless of style or preference, stories can help members of an innovation team tap into empathy and imagination . . . and ideas start flowing—even for those who aren't naturally inclined to generate ideas. Stories also promote empathetic thinking, so participants generate ideas that have more emotional context. In addition, story techniques help mitigate challenging team dynamics.

We draw on all three assessments—FourSight, Team Dimensions, and Myers-Briggs—to help us understand and manage the team dynamics that surface during collaborative work. Using insights from all of them, we boil it down to three ways stories help us manage participants with diverse styles and overcome innovation obstacles.

Serious Workers

Engineers, scientists, accountants, and people in technical professions sometimes struggle during ideation. They often play the Executors—the ones who need to produce a viable product that will work within a set of nonnegotiable constraints. They can get uncomfortable with the ambiguity associated with ideation and the unconventional and silly ideas that surface. With highly developed and dominant analytical and critical-thinking skills, they can have a hard time getting into the mood for ideation. It's not uncommon for them to be reticent and critical of the playful activities used in creative problem solving. Many are introverted and reluctant to share what they're thinking in a group. Plus, their depth of knowledge and insights can't be captured in sound bites and sticky notes, so they hold back.

Both analytical and creative thinking are needed to generate good ideas. Innovation needs the ideas that serious workers contribute, but it might be harder to draw them out in group situations. Stories can ease them into a more creative mind-set. More importantly, well-told and meaningful stories help these serious workers gain empathy and emotional insights that lead to more diverse ideas. Activities that allow serious workers time for quiet reflection after a moving story can produce high-impact ideas.

Bias-for-Action Leaders

These natural implementers who like to move the ball forward can get frustrated with the ideation process. When they see a problem, they aren't comfortable until they're chasing a solution. Regardless of their area of expertise or role on a team, these contributors push for closure and are happy when the tasks are getting done. Many corporate cultures reward this style, so it often dominates innovation teams. But these contributors can benefit from slowing down to explore ideas and possibilities before driving an idea to closure. Stories can help these team members understand that problems are complex, full of ambiguity, and fraught with human emotion.

Prolific Ideators

Give Ideators a challenge, and you'll likely get twenty-five ideas in five minutes or less. They don't need any stimulus to trigger ideation—their brains are prolific in spewing out ideas. Stories can help them when it's time to converge by illuminating the deeper meaning and universal truths that help to define the path forward. At a time in ideation where their energy wanes and they want to move on to the next idea, stories can draw them into a larger narrative that keeps them engaged. Activities in which a team develops a shared narrative (e.g., Snowball Pair and Share) will keep ideators engaged and energized.

Ways to Bring Stories into Ideation Sessions

Stories can be used in a wide range of ideation activities. During opening remarks, stories set the stage for ideation by helping participants suspend disbelief and imagine possibilities. When introducing an ideation exercise that's intended to explore emotional needs, a story can put the team into a more empathetic frame of mind. Stories also help teams extract meaning from data and generate ideas from those insights.

Prework

Before a session even begins, you can get an audience into a storytelling mind-set by having them experience or create a story. Send a short story, audio clip, or video for them to ponder as an advance assignment. Find a representative story that will take less than ten minutes to read (less than five is even better).

For a more complex task, consider assigning participants to write a three- or six-word story. Or they might share a personal story that somehow relates to the problem or challenge. It's not uncommon for participants to come without having done the assignment. Allow for this possibility while respecting those who complete it.

Silent Reading Alone

An easy way to bring a story into an ideation session is to allow two to five minutes of quiet time for participants to read a story. The story can be on a handout or a slide. Just give everyone their own space to absorb and process the story. This technique works better once a session is rolling rather than as an opener; otherwise, you risk losing your audience before you have engaged them. A silent reading just before a break can close one activity and bridge to the next.

Participant(s) Reading Out Loud

Harkening back to elementary school, you can read a story out loud to the group or have the participants read it. This technique works well when you want to use a children's book, poem, or short story. Play around with ways to rotate who is reading to engage more members of the audience and to break the potential monotony of one person reading.

Consider how to use kinesthetic techniques to stage this experience. Readers can stand while they read and then sit. Or the orators can line up in the front of the room. Give them creative license to immerse in the story and express emotion with nonverbal cues—maybe even act out what they're saying or hearing.

Group Recitation

Another easy technique is to have everyone read a story together out loud. Better yet, have them stand. Especially after lunch or during a midafternoon slump, this activity will get the blood flowing back to people's brains. Shift group dynamics by joining the audience during a recitation—it signals that the group owns the narrative, rather than the facilitator, and encourages more engagement.

Personal Stories

Share a relevant story from your life or work using your own narration skills to spin the tale. Authentic tales about struggle, triumph, and growth told in your own words can move an audience more than a fairy tale or fantasy. Real-life episodes are relatable, so we hook into the lessons and universal truths they impart. Chances are your personal story will prompt similar stories from participants and ideas will start flowing. For help with personal storytelling, refer to chapters 2 and 6, which delve into tools and techniques for finding, developing, and sharing stories in business situations.

Video or Audio Clip

In the age of the internet, you have access to a plethora of clips to share. Explore YouTube, podcasts, and the news for meaningful stories that can stimulate ideation. These stories can validate and humanize an insight by reflecting the broader culture.

Clips from audiobooks, movies, TV shows, or stand-up comedy also can shed light on a challenge. Seek stories that offer divergent perspectives and alternative realities that push participants to think outside their own experience. Look to chapter 5 for guidance on how to create multimedia story presentations.

Skit

If you and others are willing to put a little more effort into storytelling—and stretch the team's creativity—stage a skit to tell a story. Consider adding theatrical elements, even if they're rough and amateur. Cast leaders and influencers (if they'll play along) in key roles. This can be powerful because they immerse themselves in the story and put themselves in a visible—and potentially vulnerable—position. People connect with vulnerability. Embellish the skit with staging, costumes, and props. Rehearse ahead of the event. Chapter 8 provides an example of a skit and activities for an innovation working session.

Story Techniques to Diverge

Repeating stages of diverging and converging fuel all phases of innovation, but they're particularly vital during ideation. Creative problem solving is enabled when these thinking processes are separated, because a greater number of more novel ideas will surface when judgment and decision-making are suspended. To emphasize these distinct processes, the ideation techniques in this chapter are grouped into two categories: *diverge* and *converge*. When leading these exercises, look back at the ground rules of divergent thinking covered in the introduction.

Stories and story-based techniques provide wonderful stimuli for the divergent-thinking stage of ideation. Stories connect us to shared human experiences. They impart wisdom, inspiration, and universal truths. When used as inspiration for ideation, stories spark ideas that have emotional context and scalable insights.

A range of stories and story exercises can help a team unearth powerful ideas and insights to help solve problems. Company stories, user stories, or your own tales from work and life can inspire a team to think differently. Fiction, fairy tales, and fables provide lessons that reflect our shared humanity.

Company Stories

Relevant stories from founders, consumers, leaders, or employees stimulate deeper insights and more ideas. Stories also help a team view a problem from a different point of view than their own. For example, you could dig into the company's history to unearth the founder's story: their inspiration for starting the company, the struggles they overcame, the people who helped, and the leadership values the founder demonstrated. A founder story can bring the team members back to the company's roots as they think about innovation.

Empathy Stories

A story that evokes empathy around the user's point of view will inspire a team to explore more relevant and insightful possibilities. Stories that reveal universal truths that reflect our collective human condition connect with people at a visceral level. The ideas that emerge from these stories can apply to a niche or the mainstream because they're grounded in a common experience that almost everyone has undergone.

As stimuli for ideation, these stories create a mood, illuminate an insight, or reveal empathy for a user. They can be curated from user-input sessions or personal stories, brand stories, consumer stories, founder stories, employee stories, fables, books, or movies.

For example, the following empathy story was developed to train marketers in a health-care company how to communicate more effectively with women consumers, who make 80 percent of the health-care decisions for their families. The goal of this and related empathy stories was to help the marketing team understand that on the other side of a claims call someone is experiencing an emotional crisis—and that crisis often extends beyond the patient into the family.

"I Can't Believe Eric Has Diabetes"

"Mom, I'm not taking this note to my teacher," ten-year-old Eric protests while Karla shoves stuff into his backpack.

"But Eric, your teacher needs to know these details about your blood sugar."

He grabs his backpack and hollers, "Don't send any more notes to my teacher." The door slams shut.

Twelve-year-old Emily rushes into the kitchen and asks for her band shirt. Karla taps herself on the forehead: "Oh, darn—I forgot to put it in the dryer. I'm sorry! I'll bring it to school before the concert."

Emily bursts into tears. "You ruin everything! I was going to hang out with Marissa before the concert. I don't want to meet up with you." Karla reaches to hug her, but Emily wrestles away and screams, "If you weren't always obsessing about Eric's diabetes, maybe you could keep track of what I need." The sweet smell of Emily's shampoo lingers in the air after she flings her mane and turns away. The door slams again.

Karla drops into a chair and scans the kitchen. She sees the three-ring binder with activity, diet, blood sugar, and insulin charts . . . and the blood sugar kit sitting on the counter. Eric's weekly meal plan takes center stage on the fridge. It dawns on her that his diabetes is the focal point of her life. She sinks her head in her hands for a few reflective moments, then sighs and returns to her chores. "First thing is to get Emily's shirt dry."

Later, Karla gets a call from the principal. Eric got into a fight during recess with his friend Nick, who didn't want Eric on their kickball team. Eric got mad and pushed Nick down after Nick said, "You can't run fast anymore because you have diabetes." The principal asks if she and Dave can come in for a meeting with Eric's teacher and the school counselor.

During the meeting, Karla and Dave learn more about what happened on the playground. Nick had overheard his mom saying Karla was really worried Eric might overexert himself in sports and have a diabetic reaction. Nick thought that meant Eric could no longer be their best base runner.

After the meeting, Karla and Dave stop for a cup of coffee. Gently, Dave takes her hand in his. "Karen, you need to lighten up. You call the school every day. We haven't had a date night in ages, and the rare times we socialize, all you talk about is Eric's diabetes. Our friends don't care about these details. Let me help. We need to be a team."

Karla squeezes his hand as her eyes well up. "You're right. I guess this has taken over my life. I'm just so worried about Eric. There's so much to learn and manage."

"Well, we aren't the first family who's dealt with this," Dave reminds her. "There must be resources to help us." Karla nods.

"I'll look into it tomorrow."

—Jean Storlie

"I Can't Believe Eric Has Diabetes" could help other types of business challenges. A medical device company could brainstorm new technology solutions for child athletes with diabetes. Or a fitness company might invent cool gadgets to help Eric and his mom track his critical biometrics in a fun, virtual, and private way. A wellness company could generate holistic solutions to help the whole family cope with this life change.

How did Eric's story help you imagine his and his family's needs? Did you think beyond the technical and practical solutions? Did you surprise yourself with any novel ideas?

Story Box

The story box is a fast and efficient way to generate a new story based on different elements of a story structure. Scriptwriter Francis "Fran" Striker used it to create new episodes for *The Lone Ranger*, a popular radio series that began in the 1930s and became a popular television program in the 1950s. Striker constructed an elaborate chart that listed the major elements of an Old West story (e.g., good characters, bad characters, kinds of crimes, different kinds of weapons, and locations). He generated long lists of variables for each category and numbered them. Each day he'd ask a colleague for a series of random numbers (one per category). Then he'd look up the items corresponding to the random numbers chosen by his colleagues and write a new story based on those items. He didn't include a column for the moral of the story. It was the same for all episodes: good beats evil.

The story-box technique has been adopted by many screenwriters, novelists, authors, musicians, product designers, and marketers to generate entirely new ideas that are variations of an original. Think of all the examples of art and entertainment—and commercial products—that are new expressions of an existing idea. For example, the movie *Alien* (1979) is a variation of *Jaws* (1975) set in space. Country and folk songs build off tried-and-true storylines, rhythms, and chord sequences. Bike-sharing apps that have become popular in many cities are variations of Uber and Airbnb.

Simplified Story Box Analysis of *The Lone Ranger* Episodes

	Setting	Hero	Villain	Tension	Victim
1	Canyon	Lone Ranger	Bank robbers	Robbery	Bank or store owner
2	Silver mine	Tonto	Outlaws	Murder	Townspeople
3	Old bridge	Silver	Horse thief	Land dispute	Settlers
4	Main Street	U.S. marshal	Henchmen	Explosion	Innocent child
5	Miner's shack	Texas Rangers	Evil land baron	Gunfire	Damsel in distress
6	Last Chance Saloon	Pony Express	Card shark	Attack	Stagecoach passengers
7	Farmstead	Doctor	Vigilante	Love betrayal	Orphaned youth

Note: The content of this table is inspired by and adapted from materials developed by Peter Zapf of Fogpilot, a strategic brand design firm, Chicago, 2008. Used with permission.

To use this time-tested technique, create a story-box worksheet or use a flip chart with pages labeled for different parameters of the challenge.

- Specify the challenge you want to solve.
- Select the story elements (e.g., columns for mentor, ally, or moral/lesson); if a variable is fixed or irrelevant, don't include it.
- List variations or options under each story element.
- Choose the most interesting or intriguing options from each list.
- Experiment with different combinations.

The Idea Box and Morphological Analysis

Developed by Dr. Fritz Zwicky—an astrophysicist at Caltech and the "father" of jet propulsion—morphological analysis is a method to automatically combine the parameters of a challenge into new ideas. The Idea Box, a commonly used tool in creative problem solving, stems from Zwicky's morphological analysis.

In morphological analysis, you deconstruct a challenge by identifying the parameters associated with it (e.g., characteristic, factor, variable, or aspect) and placing them in column headings. To determine whether a parameter is important enough to add to the analysis, you ask, "Would the challenge still exist without this parameter?" This approach requires an additional step of divergent thinking around the parameters associated with a challenge to construct the idea box. Morphological analysis is a particularly useful strategy for putting form and structure around an amorphous challenge.

Story Box for Positioning a Nighttime Smoothie

Here's a story-box example that illustrates how a team might generate stories to help them develop a nighttime smoothie concept. They brainstorm possible settings where consumers might be relaxing before bedtime, then fill in the story box with heroes, villains, sources of tension, and morals or lessons.

Challenge Statement: How might we position a lavender-flavored yogurt smoothie?				
Setting	**Hero**	**Villain**	**Tension**	**Moral/Lesson**
Dorm room	Brand	Annoying roommate	Can't fall asleep	Sweet dreams = happy day
Family room	Friend	Noisy teenagers	Travel delays	Wake up refreshed
Hotel room	Spouse	Loud neighbors	Jet lag	Productive after a good sleep
Yoga studio	College student	Lousy airline	Can't concentrate	Bedtime rituals can pay off
Assisted living facility	Business traveler	Demanding boss	Dozing in meetings	I can soothe myself
Cabin	Scientist who invented it	Lazy coworker	Can't stay asleep	Grandma knew best
Bedroom	Chef who created it	Hotel staff	Too much work	De-stress with TLC

A variety of plots can be constructed from this story box to help the team explore ways to position a bedtime smoothie. For example, by randomly circling one choice from each column, the following plot unfolds:

A jet-lagged business traveler in a hotel room gets a call from his demanding boss that requires him to stay up late. When he finally lays down, noisy people in the room next door keep him awake. After tossing and turning, he gets up to find his earplugs. Then he remembers how his grandma took lavender-scented baths to relax. She also made him hot milk with honey when he had a bad dream.

More variations can be added and combined to create other plots that range from the obvious to the outlandish. The plots created from a story box help a team imagine possibilities and explore a challenge from different angles.

Improv: Pass the Plot

Improvisation is a playful way to get a team freewheeling with story creation, and it gives people permission to play. We use Pass the Plot to encourage participants to think about plot development through an improv approach. This technique leads to ad-lib story creation, with each participant contributing one element to a plot.

Form a line or circle with five to seven participants. Supply the first plot point: the setup. The first participant thickens the plot, then passes the story to the next person to build on the plot as shown in the accompanying diagram. You can prompt partipants using cues from the diagram to keep them on track and the game moving.

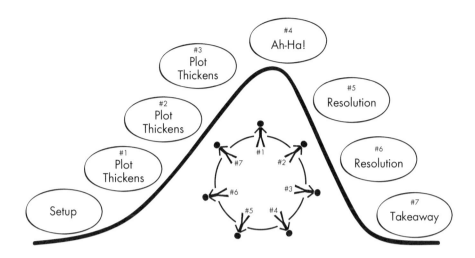

Campfire Story Circles

This technique, which was introduced in chapter 3 as a technique to help a team extract meaning out of data and insights, can be used in ideation in much the same way. Instead of structuring the circle discussions to help a team gain empathy and clarify insights, use campfire circles during ideation to spark the flow of ideas and get participants in a freewheeling mood. Simulate the spontaneous energy that campfires ignite. Start by sharing a story or story prompt and, like kindling on a fire, soon their stories will flow naturally. After campfire story sharing in small groups for five to ten minutes, lead the team through an idea-generating exercise and capture the ideas on sticky notes, flip-chart paper, or a worksheet. Chances are the ideas will be imaginative and rich with emotional context.

As a stimulus for ideation, the campfire story sharing can be related to the challenge or random and free flowing. We like to use challenge-oriented story circles to open an ideation (i.e., during a first or second round of ideation). The freewheeling, random approach is a great energizer before a forced-connections exercise in a third round of ideation.

Guided Imagery Plus a Story

This technique was first introduced and described in chapter 2 as a visioning tool. In chapter 3, we provided modifications for using this technique in exploration and clarification. Guided imagery, along with a story, also works as stimulus for ideation. After taking participants into a meditative state, read a short children's book, poem, fable, or folk tale. A poignant user story might also work. Select a story that illuminates a universal truth related to the challenge.

Story Techniques to Converge

After diverging to generate a long list of ideas, it's time to converge and make choices. We've both participated in hour-long ideation sessions that spend fifty-five minutes freewheeling on idea generation. Then in the final five minutes, when everyone is ready to file out of the room toward their next task, the meeting organizer asks everyone to place a dot next to ideas they like. In that situation, no time has been allotted for an effective converge phase, which effectively squanders all the time spent generating ideas. In fact, converging should occupy at least the same amount of time spent diverging.

In the converge phase of ideation, we seek to curate a "portfolio of ideas" that range from the obvious and viable ideas to the zany-yet-intriguing ones produced during diverge. During converge, a team needs to be deliberate but not too judgmental. They must consolidate the plethora of ideas generated into rough concepts that can go into the develop phase, where they are strengthened into fully developed, viable concepts. Story techniques, along with analytical tools, can help them do that. After ideas are sorted and clustered to find themes, a range of story techniques can help a team turn ideas into concepts.

Roving Conversations Meets Build-a-Story

Roving Conversations is a kinesthetic activity in which groups of two to three rotate to flip-chart stations where they contribute to a problem-solving task. In this highly flexible technique, stations are designed for participants to add new ideas, critique possible solutions, and cluster ideas into broader themes. As illustrated below, Roving Conversations enables team members to draft and edit stories by building on each other's work. When the goal is to create a collection of shared narratives, this technique works well because everyone contributes to all the stories, which are polished by small work groups. Before this exercise commences, the team should be aligned on three to five broad themes or pillars that will be used as a springboard for developing stories. Designate one flip chart for each theme.

Through the groups' contributions to drafting and editing multiple stories, everyone gains ownership of these shared narratives. The accompanying table provides an example of how to structure this activity to solve a hypothetical challenge: Write a story about how athletes use sports performance products. In this example, the teams are named after mythical creatures (which are more playful than numbers). The teams rotate through four stations that represent categories of sports performance products.

Building a Story with the Roving Conversations Technique

	Station 1	**Station 2**	**Station 3**	**Station 4**
Strategic Pillar, Theme, or Category	Strength	Endurance	Weight Loss	Speed and Power
Round 1: Start • Ideate story ideas • Pick one • Sketch out plot	Team Dragon	Team Mermaid	Team Fairy	Team Unicorn
Round 2: Refine • Refine plot • Develop characters • Add vivid details	Team Unicorn	Team Dragon	Team Mermaid	Team Fairy
Round 3: Refine • Refine plot • Add vivid details • Streamline	Team Fairy	Team Unicorn	Team Dragon	Team Mermaid
Round 4: Return to Start • Return to first station • Create draft #2 • Prepare to share	Team Dragon	Team Mermaid	Team Fairy	Team Unicorn

During the first round, the teams brainstorm possible stories that exemplify the theme and then select the best story idea. They sketch out the story's plot on the flip chart. After twenty to thirty minutes, the groups rotate to the next station, where they have five to ten minutes to build on the story drafted by the preceding group. They clarify confusion, modify plot points, and bring the characters and setting to life with pictures and vivid details. This process is repeated at the third station. (If you're short on time, you could truncate to one round of editing.)

After two to three editing rotations, teams return to their original stations. They review the input other groups offered about their original story idea and create a second draft. Provide access to visual aids (e.g., magazines, clip art, or photo decks) to help them develop a more refined story and get ready to share it with the whole group. Allow thirty to forty-five minutes for this step.

During the debrief, invite each team to share their story. We like to give participants flexibility to express the story in their own creative style—they may read it, act it out, or narrate it. Probe for input to improve on their story draft. Ask participants if this story inspires any other story ideas that could convey the same insight and idea.

Because participants are moving around and actively working in teams, this activity can overcome the postlunch slump. It's most successful with two or three people per team. When the teams have more than four, some participants will disengage and the team may struggle to align on the decisions they need to make.

Six-Word Stories

According to urban legend, Ernest Hemingway was once challenged in a bar to write a story in six words. To settle the bet, he wrote, "For sale: baby shoes, never worn." He won the bet and believed that this story was his best work. At the same time, he created a challenge for generations of future writers and storytellers.

Much evidence points to the possibility that this tale may not be true, but it brilliantly illustrates that even radically short stories can carry meaning. A story told in six words requires active participation on the part of the listener because we have to think about it, ask questions, and even discuss it to "get it." Only then can we draw conclusions about the storyteller, the story line, or even the outcome.

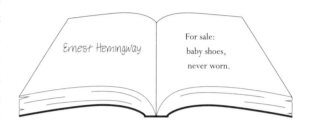

Six-word-story exercises can be used in many problem-solving situations, but they're particularly effective during convergence. A team selects four to six stories that represent the best insights, ideas, and experiences related to the project. Then they craft six-word stories that capture each story's essence. A picture plus a six-word story can depict the essence of an insight or idea. Perhaps that's why memes have become so prevalent.

Coupling a six-word story and photo with a longer narrative as backup might be useful when pitching and engaging stakeholders. A collection of six-word stories that represent strategic pillars or the team's journey can help the team unify around sound bites and key messages for stakeholder communications (see chapters 6 and 7 for more tools about pitching with stories).

Snowball Pair and Share

The Snowball Pair and Share activity introduced in chapter 2 can be used to get a team to converge around strong ideas and representative stories. Before developing stories, the team sorts and assimilates ideas into broad themes. Then each participant selects one theme they find inspiring. Participants work alone for five to ten minutes to develop stories related to their themes. In the next round, participants pair up and share their stories. Pairs join with other pairs to share their stories, refining and building on each other's narratives.

Closing Thoughts

Natural ideators spew ideas as easily as they breathe. The rest of us need some warming up to get into a creative mind-set and start generating ideas. Neuroscience reveals that the brain centers associated with creativity are very responsive to relaxation and play. Stories entertain, relax, and transport us to imaginary places. The combination of a story with guided imagery is a very powerful duo to get people into creative flow.

Stories can help serious workers be a little more playful and imaginative. They also help the hard-chargers slow down and reflect. Lastly, stories help natural ideators focus their energy. Some people need quiet reflection, while others need interaction to get their ideas flowing. Stories lend themselves to both individual and group activities.

As Mimi learned from her intern, there's a time and a place for divergent thinking and not everyone appreciates a brain dump of ideas. The yin to idea generation is the yang of convergence. Teams need to spend equal amounts of time diverging and converging to decide which ideas to keep exploring and which ones to set aside. If the converge process is random and unfocused (e.g., dot voting as people leave the room) or too rigid and judgmental, the fruits of ideation won't be harvested.

Stories often have many ideas and meanings. They can help generate ideas and also converge on broad themes and universal truths. We believe great ideas solve human problems, and the best way to think about human problems is through stories.

The most beautiful world is always entered through imagination.
—Helen Keller

5

Develop, Test, and Prototype with Stories

Stories bring promising ideas to life for testing and refinement

"We Love This Idea!"
By Mimi Sherlock

Rick assembled the product team to brief them on a new sales opportunity he'd identified. An iconic clothing retailer that caters to wealthy women aged forty and beyond had posted a request for proposals (known as an RFP) to develop and supply an exclusive perfume for their customers. It would be the first fragrance offering for this large retailer. Landing this contract with a successful product offering would drive incremental growth for their company (a boutique fragrance supplier).

Shaniqua, the marketing manager, and Tara, the consumer insights associate, arrived together. They got excited about the opportunity when Rick shared key passages from the RFP. Jacques, the master perfumer who led product development, slid in a few minutes late. He perked up once he grasped the scope and scale of the opportunity.

As the team combed through the RFP, they flagged a few challenges. It was a fast-track project, and they anticipated stiff competition. The brief described the customer's vision to brand a "fresh" and "distinctive" scent, and it detailed numerous requirements about packaging, sourcing, and cost. But it lacked clarity about the sensory characteristics that typically guide fragrance development.

Without clear guardrails, the young women on the team convinced Jacques to pursue an exotic direction that appealed to their taste as individuals. He got excited about this creative direction. A few weeks later, he'd produced a prototype the team loved.

They met The Golden Nose (the person "smelling" for the client company) in the lobby and immediately connected with her. Warm and bubbly, she was new to her role. She exuded excitement about the scent: "Our company has such a subdued style, but this product could really stretch us." The team left feeling confident about their pitch.

Three weeks later, they were shocked when The Golden Nose called with bad news: the product had failed miserably in consumer testing. Two competitors had produced winning concepts. Rick and his team were out!

When Development Goes Sideways

In this fictionalized scenario, Tara and Shaniqua led Jacques down a flawed creative path because they were designing for their tastes, not the upscale, middle-aged-and-older women who comprised the target user. Rick went along with his colleagues' idea, excited that they were putting their creative energy into this potentially lucrative opportunity. Jacques was inspired by the challenge of creating an exotic fragrance.

The team skipped key steps in their race to execution. They didn't take time to clarify the challenge, understand the user, or test their assumptions. Instead they acted on their first idea and formulated a prototype for the wrong audience. This story illustrates one way innovation can go sideways during development, but teams can encounter other landmines when navigating the ambiguity of the development-and-testing phase (the CPS model calls it the *develop phase*).

This chapter explores how idea development can veer off track and how stories can help teams navigate this phase of innovation. User stories are particularly useful during idea development. Compelling written and oral narratives add clarity to briefing sessions and bring concepts and prototypes to life. We also delve into the principles of Design Thinking, a human-centered innovation model that emphasizes empathy and iterative prototyping along with end-user feedback. We share a range of story-based techniques and storytelling skills to enhance idea development testing and prototyping, and we offer guidance on how to curate and retell user stories.

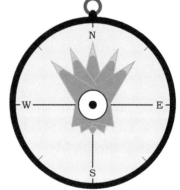

Staying on Course

All stages of innovation involve navigating ambiguity, setting a clear vision, plotting a path, and staying on track. At the same time, teams need to adjust the course as new information emerges during development. Feedback and learning is important, but irrelevant input and tangents can throw leaders and teams off course.

As an idea turns into a concept—then later a prototype and, eventually, a finished product—sometimes each step strays from the original idea. It's like the whispering game telephone, when a beginning idea often morphs into an entirely different product. Unguided iteration produces "warm tea" (i.e., neither soothingly hot nor refreshingly cold). Without careful attention, an idea can be diluted into something that means nothing.

Successful innovation leaders navigate the development phase by accurately and consistently conveying the core essence of an idea so everyone who touches the concept in development is aiming toward the same goal and knows what to do to get there. They also provide creative guidance—with guardrails—so executors produce accurate representations (visuals and prototypes) of the idea.

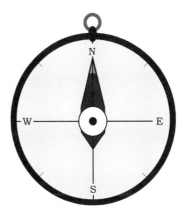

A green light to test a proof of concept usually includes some funding but also a short leash. Teams often face time and resource constraints to develop and test. If execution teams misunderstand the concept or take too much creative license of their own, they'll produce a misguided prototype, which might fail consumer tests. When prototypes and tests fail to deliver on the expectations framed in the original pitch, stakeholder support evaporates. In the worst-case scenario, a project blows up in complete failure.

Focus on the pivotal insight—think of it as the true north that guides development. If the pivotal insight fails in early testing, be deliberate in choosing a new compass point. Go back to the core user stories to get reoriented. Successful innovation leaders keep themselves and their execution teams focused on the correct compass point.

How Stories Can Keep Development on Track

When development teams misunderstand the essential elements of an idea, they may produce a flawed prototype or product, which wastes time and money. A representative story can help keep everyone who touches the product development moving in the same direction.

Stories Refine and Advance High-Potential Ideas

When technical experts favor different ideas than the marketing and insights professionals, teams experience conflict. We use a feasibility-potential map to dissipate that dynamic. This exercise engages the team in a collaborative, deliberate process of sorting and scoring ideas. Then it uses story techniques to refine the ideas to improve the technical feasibility and marketplace potential.

This exercise involves a two-by-two matrix with technical and scientific feasibility on one axis and consumer and marketplace potential on the other. The process of scoring and plotting ideas on the matrix harmonizes decision-making within the team. This works particularly well for consumer-oriented products that have a scientific or technical basis, such as foods, household appliances, and personal electronics.

We break out the marketing and technical teams into separate groups. The marketing and insights

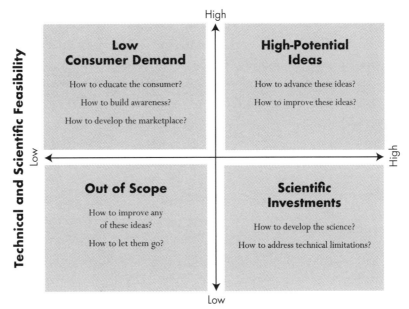

team members score all the ideas for consumer and marketplace potential while the technical experts do the same with technical feasibility using the Concept Creator Score Card. Then they collaborate as a large group to plot the ideas on the Feasibility-Potential Matrix. Once all the ideas are placed in the four quadrants, they discuss ways to refine and improve on the ideas.

After the large group aligns on the high-potential ideas, we rearrange it into cross-functional teams of three to five participants who take one to three high-potential ideas and use story techniques to develop the ideas into fleshed-out concepts. They might create a skit, draw a storyboard, or use a collage or 3-D model to share their narrative with the team. This exercise takes a few hours but often produces well-developed, viable concepts. The final presentations also serve as a capstone to the working session. Consider inviting executives and stakeholders to join during this part.

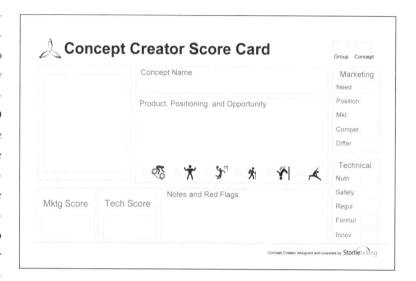

Stories Enable Human-Centered Design (Design Thinking)

Empathy is the centerpiece of human-centered design, or Design Thinking, which is a creative problem solving method that has been slowly evolving since the 1950s. Design Thinking was popularized for business purposes and nondesigners in the 1990s by the consulting firm IDEO, famous for designing iconic products like the iPhone. The Hasso Plattner Institute of Design at Stanford University (better known today as *Stanford d.school*) started teaching Design Thinking in 2005, and it's now widely used as a methodology for innovation.

User stories fuel human-centered design. They enable empathy, problem definition, ideation, and prototype design and iteration. Stories punch up these prototypes by providing more emotional context and insight. Crude prototypes become a prop for the story rather than the main vehicle for communicating the idea.

Design Thinking employs consumer personas to evoke empathy, but we believe that going one step further by creating consumer or user narratives is even more powerful. When developers understand not just the user's personality but also their human struggles, they can better address both emotional and functional needs. More creative solutions will result from this deeper understanding. (See appendix A for additional background on Design Thinking models and key principles.)

Consumer Narratives

In chapter 3 we introduce the Continuum for Presenting Consumer Data with Narrative Elements. We emphasize the value of going beyond consumer profiles and personas that characterize and personify a consumer target to create consumer narratives that tell a story about the consumer's emotional struggles.

Sometimes developers and vendors will append briefs with consumer research reports, but often briefing documents simply include a bulleted list of attributes that profile the consumer. Sometimes they include a persona that brings the consumer to life with a name, picture, and first-person statements. Incorporating consumer narratives in briefing documents further humanizes the target user and brings greater clarity to development teams. Let's go back to the story "We Love This Idea!" and compare and contrast the different approaches that might be used in briefing documents. Consider a spectrum of options for sharing background on the target user of the new perfume.

Continuum of Consumer Briefing Options

Consumer Profile	Consumer Persona	Consumer Narrative
• 40+ years old • Upscale buyer • Exquisite taste • Classy, elegant, expensive • Wealthy elite • Part of the country-club set • Executive and/or political circles	I'm Susan. My wardrobe reflects my preference for making an exquisite versus a flashy statement. I seek understated, elegant styles. I'll pay top dollar for high-quality clothing that I'll wear for years rather than trendy pieces that will go out of style after one season. I want first-rate fabrics and workmanship. When shopping, I want to be catered to. I don't want to feel ordinary.	"Susan's Horrible Shopping Trip" (see accompanying story)

Consumer Narrative: Susan's Horrible Shopping Trip

Susan pulled her dress out of her suitcase and was horrified to discover a large stain down the front. "There's no way I can wear this dress to my niece's wedding. How did I miss that stain when I packed last night?" After six hours of traveling, she'd just arrived at a remote sea village on the coast of Maine. She looked at her diamond-studded watch, "Yikes—four hours before family pictures!" Her husband had just left with their rental car to visit his mother. Instead of luxuriating in the bath and taking a nap, she shrugged off the plush robe she'd donned moments earlier and jumped back into her clothes. Ten minutes later she was in a cab on her way to the rundown shopping mall she'd seen when they drove into town. All the quaint little boutiques on Main Street were shuttered in the off-season.

Pawing through crowded rack of cheap dresses, she thought, "No wonder I never shop in department stores. ... Who gets married on a Sunday?... Why do they have to hold their wedding in the middle of nowhere?" Hoping to get some assistance, she approached a clerk at the register in the Women's Dresses department. "Good Lord, she has purple hair and a nose ring! What does she know about fashion?"

In a huff, Susan asked the clerk where higher-quality merchandise could be found—and named a few high-end brands. She wanted to scream when the clerk gave her an empty stare and shrugged, "Everything we have is out on the floor." Her disinterest was too much! Susan's nerves snapped. Before she could think, she vented all her frustrations on the dismayed clerk.

When Susan turned to storm away, another customer gently tapped her arm. "I'm sorry, but I couldn't help but overhear your horrible predicament. I can't imagine how stressful it must be to find a suitable dress for a family wedding on such short notice." Susan blushed, embarrassed that she'd made a scene, while she took in this classy, genteel woman. The stranger continued, "I live here, but usually shop in Boston for my clothes. I might be able to help you. I know the owner of a boutique in town. She goes to my church, and I just saw her this morning. I'll see if she'd be willing to open her shop for you. I'll drive you there. I'm going that way."

Desperate, Susan accepted this kind offer from the complete stranger. Thirty minutes later, she was trying on dresses in a charming, exquisitely decorated shop. The owner had pulled out three gorgeous dresses and quietly waited, ready to assist. Susan exhaled her anxiety and thought, "This is my kind of store." A half hour later, with a new dress, shoes, and accessories, she was back in a cab. A glance at her watch showed that she had ninety minutes before pictures. Phew! Crisis averted.

—Jean Storlie

When you read Susan's story, what do you understand about her that you don't get from the profile and persona? How might this story have helped the team develop a perfume that would appeal to Susan? Do you need to like Susan to understand her?

This story leaves some readers frustrated that Susan got away with out-of-bounds behavior. Her tension was resolved, but their feelings about justice and decency were not. How might Susan get a comeuppance?

Stories Bring Greater Clarity to Briefing Sessions

Creative, project, and technical briefing documents guide execution teams as they bring concepts to life through visual and physical representations. Innovation leaders might oversee artistic and technical teams as they create renditions that illustrate a product's features and benefits. A relevant story that illuminates a key insight or portrays how the product solves a user's problem can be included in a briefing document to help others gain empathy and understanding.

Sift through the insights from interactions with users, as well as other materials collected during the exploration and clarification phase to find grist for developing the characters, plot, and central tension. If you created consumer narratives, they might be useful to include. Play around with the story-box ideation tool to generate possible story elements, then mix and match these elements to develop a plot (i.e., setting, hero, villain, tension, and moral or lesson).

You don't need to create advertising copy to sharpen a brief. Simply think about brand stories and the roles that products play in their customers' lives when selecting stories for a brief.

Product as a Hero

Many marketing campaigns depict a product swooping in (as the hero) to save the day for the consumer (as the victim). These narratives are grounded in the universal plot that stems from fairy tales with three main characters: a victim, a villain, and a hero. The villain might come from an adversarial person or situation, or an internal struggle the victim faces. Joseph Campbell, a literary theorist and myth expert, describes a hero as "someone who has given his or her life to something bigger than themselves." A hero might be a warrior, savior, underdog, or ordinary person. Nike is an iconic hero brand: it aims to transform the average person into a champion. Articulating the ways your product idea stands for a higher purpose will help you form a useful narrative about it.

Product as a Mentor

With consumers becoming more sophisticated, resourceful, and skeptical, the brand-as-a-hero story is less appealing. They perceive brands that attempt to control or dominate them as arrogant. In an influential 2014 *Adweek* article, marketing strategist Gaston Legorburu argues that brands need to let go of playing the hero and get better at playing the mentor. In that scenario, think of a brand as Glinda the Good Witch, who mentors Dorothy (the hero) in *The Wizard of Oz*. This archetype appeals to the human desire to play heroic roles and keeps the spotlight on the customer.

Story Techniques for Development and Testing

Stories can help develop, test, and refine concepts in a variety of ways. When moving an idea from a concept to a prototype to a finished product, a user story can inform the product design and development. Stories about how users react to early concepts help validate and refine preliminary ideas and concepts. Stories can play a vital role in the process of developing, testing, and refining that nurtures innovation.

Bringing a Concept to Life

Prototypes allow users to experience a product concept. Stories help them imagine what it might do for them. The combination of the two will help users better understand how a product can help them, and, in turn, the users will provide more practical and relevant feedback.

Visual + Story

Pictures plus a consumer profile or persona often accompany briefing documents. Take it a step further and build the persona into a narrative. If you crafted consumer narratives during the clarify phase, resurrect them.

Develop a narrative that shows how the "persona" struggles and transforms. Keep refining the story as you gather more user feedback and understanding. Be scrappy about finding images. Take your own pictures. Search for images in the public domain (Pixabay, Unsplash, and Creative Commons offer searchable collections of free images). Purchase inexpensive stock images. A professional photo shoot during prototyping and testing is unnecessary.

Prototype + Story

A prototype helps a user experience a concept; a story helps them imagine its possibilities. The best way to help others understand how a prototype works is to demonstrate it. By adding a story, you help your users imagine how it might solve their problems. On the back end of a prototype test, stories about users' experience with the prototype will inform further refinement. The combination of prototypes plus stories brings concepts to life in a robust way.

**A prototype helps a user experience a concept;
a story helps them imagine its possibilities.**

Curating User Stories

Relevant consumer stories inform product design, marketing, messaging, and ongoing development. Draw inspiration from consumer profiles and segmentation data, but go a few steps further. Explore common story elements that reflect not just one person's story but the whole consumer group's shared narrative. Bring it to life with specific characters, setting, plot points, and resolution. To develop a rich narrative, you may need to curate several user stories before universal truths and broad themes come into focus.

User stories emerge from ethnographic work completed during exploration and clarification. Refer to the sidebar on ethnography in chapter 3 for more background on how this research can be turned into stories.

How to Prompt Users to Tell Stories

Use listening techniques to facilitate story sharing from users. Chapter 3 includes guidelines for story listening and appendix C provides an interview guide for eliciting stories. Ask open-ended questions that prompt a story, such as "Tell me a story about a time when …" Probe for salient details and plot elements. Show empathy as you explore a user's struggles and emotional journey. Ask why and invite the speaker to share more details with an invitation like "Show me how …" Notice something about the person, and tie that observation to the product or service you're developing.

Terry Gross of NPR's *Fresh Air* is an extremely talented interviewer who draws out her guest's stories. She often starts her interviews with the invitation "Tell me about yourself." As her guests reveal their stories, Terry connects with them by showing empathy and insights about their struggles. As she gains trust, Terry asks probing, gently worded questions. Guests respond because she makes them feel safe and understood. When interviewing users, try to be like Terry Gross.

How to Capture User Stories

When feasible, ethnographic studies or face-to-face interviews get you closest to the user. You can read body language and pick up on emotional signals that amplify (or contradict) what a user says. In-person interviews facilitate connection, trust, and rapport, which help interviewees open up and share deeper emotions. Be prepared to bear witness to someone's story if they decide to unload on you. Try to get permission to record the interview so you can be more present in the moment. A recording also provides documentation that will help you stitch the story together later.

Video conference calls are the next best method because you can observe behavior and body language. During phone interviews, you build rapport through dialogue and can still probe for deeper understanding. Again, listen to Terry Gross—many of her interviews are by phone.

You can also gather stories that include emotional context and narrative elements through online surveys. It's a more challenging method because many people aren't skilled at storytelling without some prompting. When constructing the survey, use the questioning techniques described in the story listening discussion in chapter 3, get to the heart of their experience, and gather salient details.

Retelling User Stories

For user stories to be useful during development and testing, you need to package them into coherent tales and select the right medium for sharing them. Your goal is to help people imagine the user as a character. In high school literature classes, we were taught that characters reveal themselves through *what they say, what they do,* and *what others say about them.* Try applying these same ideas to how you portray a user's character. Also consider his or her struggles as you develop the plot.

One of the many choices a storyteller makes is determining from whose perspective a story will be told. The first person or the third-person limited work well for user stories, but consider experimenting with others.

Choosing the Voice for a Story

- **First person:** The story is told from the perspective of one character who narrates what he or she thinks, feels, and experiences. This is an active voice that lends itself well to personal and business storytelling.
  Pronouns: I, me

- **Second person:** This voice, in which the narrator addresses "you," works well for instructional materials, but it isn't an appealing voice for storytelling. (We use this voice throughout *Once Upon an Innovation* when explaining how to use various tools and techniques.)
  Pronouns: you, we

- **Third person:** The story is told from the perspective of one observer who narrates using characters' names along with the pronouns "he," "she," "they," and "them." All of the third-person options can work well for storytelling.
  Pronouns: she, he, they

- **Third-person limited:** The narrator follows one character in the story. We experience events as that character would—and we learn that character's thoughts and feelings. Mysteries and thrillers often use third-person limited, and many novels shift which character we're following in different chapters.

- **Third-person objective:** The narrator tells the story as an observer who doesn't have access to any of the character's thoughts or feelings. Journalists rely on this approach, in combination with first-person quotes, to tell real-life stories.

- **Third-person omniscient:** The narrator knows the thoughts and feelings of all the characters in the story.

You also have to make a choice about telling one user's story or creating an amalgamation of multiple users' stories. To craft an amalgamation, you might develop the character based on one user but add dialogue from another and an experience or episode from a third. Stitch together these pieces into a coherent story with a plot that represents their shared experience. As you synthesize a group of users' stories, the common themes might be expressed through archetypes and universal plots.

Archetypes and universal plots might help you synthesize themes from user stories into a plot structure. David Hutchens's *Circle of the 9 Muses*, which maps out sixteen universal plots, is an excellent resource—as discussed in chapter 1.

Oral Storytelling

We hope this book inspires you to develop oral storytelling skills for business settings. Once you master these skills, stories can be brought into many leadership moments associated with innovation. Becoming skilled at oral storytelling will set you apart from other leaders and equip you with a tool that can be used in planned and spontaneous ways.

For those who want to immerse themselves in the oral storytelling tradition, the annual National Storytelling Festival in Jonesborough, Tennessee, is the mecca. Regional storytelling festivals and local theater classes are other ways to gain skills in the dramatic and entertaining side of oral storytelling. But you can also gain skills by just jumping in and starting to tell stories in casual conversations as well as in formal settings. The more you practice, the better you'll become.

Written Storytelling

The written word can be as powerful as the spoken word to convey a story. We include many stories in this book that are examples for how to write stories that illuminate your message. Selecting the voice and developing the plot provide the structure. Use dialogue, vivid description, action verbs, and sensory details to make your stories pop.

Clips from User Interactions

Both video and audio clips from users can help tell a story. Some agencies and firms provide turnkey services to produce polished multimedia stories from user clips. But if you have limited funds, you can do it yourself with PowerPoint or iMovie.

Play with the spectrum of PowerPoint's multimedia tools (graphics, animation, audio, and video), but stay away from bullet points when telling a story. Use PowerPoint as a visual aid to support your own authentic storytelling—don't use it as a crutch. One of its advantages is its availability on most desktop devices, and it has good compatibility between PC and Mac operating systems. Also, slides created in PowerPoint easily slot into bigger presentation decks.

iMovie works better for creating a slideshow out of pictures and video. The software makes it simple to add and edit underscoring with music clips.

When doing it yourself, the first step is to comb through the clips to find grist for telling the story. Perhaps one user told a vivid story that really nails a key insight or universal truth. We'll call those "hero clips." In selecting them, look for a segment that reveals a user's personality as well as the struggle, pivotal insight, and change or transformation. You may need to fill in missing elements to clarify, streamline, or provide necessary context. Be careful not to twist the truth with your edits—you need to stay true to the user's story for it to accurately guide development.

If you can't find one representative story but see a story emerge from a collection of users' inputs, you can stitch together individual clips into a shared story. This might take a little more effort but can be very effective because the story is told from a variety of viewpoints. First, look for a common experience among users. Then find clips that show the different elements of the plot: setup, rising tension, turning point, resolution, and lesson or takeaway. Add transitional commentary through the voice of an omnipotent narrator (you or a colleague with a resonant reading voice) who knows all the characters' experiences.

Audio Enhancements

Spice up story presentations with sound effects or music. Consider how musical interludes might accent the story. For example, music can help set the stage by creating a mood or capturing attention. Or you could close a story on a musical note. Alternatively, sound effects or music might help to punctuate a dramatic moment or help during transitions.

Stories in PPCo Analysis

To avoid premature idea killing, Diane Foucar-Szocki, Bill Shepard, and Roger Firestien designed and tested PPC (which stands for *pluses*, *potentials*, and *concerns*) in 1982 to develop and refine ideas. They drew from Aristotle, who believed it was vital to examine the pros and cons of any idea. Hedria Lunken evolved this method by adding a step—*overcoming concerns*—which tacked on a lowercase *o*, making it PPC*o*. This last step is brainstorming ways to overcome each concern. PPCo starts with praise, then strengthens an idea through analysis and refinement.

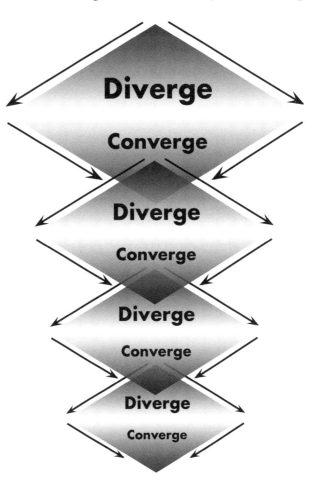

Pluses

Find three or more positive attributes and strengths about the idea. Seek to find what is good and potentially unique about the idea in its current form. Be mindful that some team members stepped out of their comfort zone to offer the idea.

Potentials

Explore the possibilities inside of each idea. List at least three opportunities that this idea might generate. Allow for spin-off and speculation—you can rein in crazy ideas later. Allow your imagination to consider possible future situations where this idea might have a place. Stories can help the team relax, be emotionally present, and imagine possibilities.

Concerns

No idea is perfect, so look for flaws and weaknesses. Build a list of concerns with input from members of the team. Ask other colleagues and stakeholders to critique. It's much better to discover design flaws during the prototyping stage than in the final stages of launch. Create a culture where it's safe for everyone to express their doubts and concerns. If people hold back their criticism for the sake of harmony, critical flaws can be swept under the rug.

Overcoming Concerns

Explore ways to overcome the limitations of an idea. Reframe concerns into creative challenges through questions that begin with phrases like "How might we . . ." and "In what ways might we . . . ." These prompts invite solutions for how to overcome each concern and avoid negative, critical language.

Through all this analysis, keep the target user in mind—view the product or service from their vantage point. It's generally not feasible to drill into this thorough analysis for each and every idea, but is an extremely valuable approach to exploring high-potential ideas.

PPCo + Story

We like to combine PPCo with story prompts to keep the imagination active while critiquing ideas. Story prompts put participants into an imaginative mind-set. Try using the prompt "What we see ourselves doing is…" Then have participants answer that question in a narrative, writing the story as a group to ensure they have alignment on the initial idea.

After completing the PPCo analysis, ask the group members to use their new insights to make the idea even stronger. Then they build on the original narrative to articulate the new and improved idea through the prompt *"Now what we see ourselves doing is…"* We believe that a combination of critical analysis and story prompting produces refined ideas.

Using Stories during Implementation

As prototypes get more refined through iterative feedback and analysis, development eventually moves into implementation. We're not dedicating a chapter to the CPS Implement phase, because there are more limited applications for story techniques during this stage. But that doesn't mean there are none. Here are our approaches and ideas for how stories can keep the momentum going once an innovation advances to implementation.

Action Planning

Some people have great ideas but don't know how to execute them. Others stop using creative problem solving processes after they've come up with a promising idea. Many are inclined to approach action planning with an analytical mind-set that prevents them from exploring novel ways to execute. It's easy to get stuck in linear thinking as you define goals, timelines, and milestones. But creative thinking can help solve the glitches and hiccups that occur during implementation.

We believe both analytical and creative approaches aid implementation, especially when used in a synergistic combination. Also, teams can accelerate execution if they continue to diverge and converge as they bring their ideas to fruition. Story-based techniques, alongside implementation tools, can help teams stay engaged in the creative process during execution. To make action planning a little more imaginative, we use two story techniques: storyboarding and backward stories.

Storyboarding

The storyboarding tool pictured in Chapter 2 can be applied to action planning in a similar way it's used for visioning. The team members develop a story that reveals the perfect ending to their innovation journey. They use vivid language to describe all the events and components associated with a successful product launch (e.g., product, packaging, website, advertising and marketing, sales materials, PR, corporate communications, distribution, logistics, and operations). With the end goal in mind, they identify the work streams that will be required to achieve this happy ending and use storyboards to map out each of them.

Backward Stories

A variation of storyboarding, the team members use guided imagery to visualize a perfect ending to their innovation story. Then they write stories that work backward to connect the ending to the current state. They can use a storyboard, a narrative arc, or action-planning tools to connect the dots.

Monitoring and Continuous Improvement

The teams on the front line of sales and customer service witness user stories that can provide a temperature gauge about how an innovation is performing in the marketplace. If the innovation is a consumer-facing product or service, monitoring what users are saying on social media provides a real-time feedback loop. An entire industry of "social listening" has emerged to monitor social media engagement and distill a bigger story from the collection of posts.

Sometimes stories help diagnose why performance is deviating from expectations, which can lead to making necessary adjustments. Or stories may validate a commercial success. We encourage innovators to continue to use story listening, synthesizing, and retelling tools to monitor the success of products, services, and programs they launch. While stories don't tick a box in the context of a traditional dashboard of performance metrics, they offer a meaningful way to contextualize and interpret data.

Closing Thoughts

The space shuttle *Challenger* wouldn't have blown up if members of the NASA development team had been courageous enough to point out their concerns about the fatal flaw on the O-ring. Development isn't a time to "go along to get along." It's a time to explore possibilities, but it's also a time to think critically, flag technical flaws, and test whether or not solutions will work for users.

Innovation gurus espouse the concept of "failing fast." Design Thinking pushes development teams to get comfortable with failure and "grow a thick skin" during the back-and-forth process of hands-on development. Criticism is a gift not a curse. Build a crude prototype, put it in front of users, and get user feedback to keep refining. Day-to-day innovation happens in small steps, not giant leaps. Stories coupled with prototypes can enable a more robust expression of the concept and enhance the quality of user input.

Taking the time to turn consumer data and insights into consumer narratives is worthwhile. These stories help keep stakeholders engaged. More importantly, they clarify and bring emotional context for vendors and development teams, who transform ideas into refined concepts, then prototypes and eventually finished products. As you pull together stories that portray your projects in a holistic way, review the tips in this chapter for crafting user stories and refer to the resources in chapter 1.

A lot of diverging and converging takes place during development, with each iteration getting more and more refined. We like the PPCo analysis tool to collect feedback for refining, especially the discipline of pointing out positives and potentials first. This keeps creative energy flowing and discourages the tendency to kill ideas prematurely.

If you want to learn more about Design Thinking, Stanford d.school offers a free online ninety-minute crash course, a six-day training workshop, and college credits in Design Thinking.

To avoid criticism, say nothing, do nothing, be nothing.
—Aristotle

6

Strategic Framing for Stakeholders

How to present a strategy through the narrative arc

"What's the Story?" Part 1
By Jean Storlie

While working with an innovation team through an intense month of immersion and ideation to develop a new product pipeline, I observed that the team was in a rocky place about the next steps in their project. Like most deep dives, the process had surfaced new questions and many possibilities. After collecting and reviewing valuable marketplace, consumer, competitor, and technical data, the team had generated a plethora of ideas. But the project was at the messy stage of how to translate all the data and insights into an actionable strategy. Team members weren't aligned on next steps, and we had one week to define the path forward and create a pitch for senior executives.

Looking out the window of the conference room, I saw the setting sun and traffic piling up on the freeway. It was Valentine's Day, and everyone was anxious for the offsite meeting to conclude so they could get on with their evenings. My consulting engagement was winding down after facilitating this one-day working session. In follow-up, I needed to assimilate their work and draft an executive pitch. My opportunity to work with the whole team was at an end. I was flying home that evening and would wrap up the project from afar.

The innovation leader was excited about the insights and ideas that had surfaced during discovery: her natural curiosity and analytical tendencies inspired her to continue sifting through the data for answers. Members of the team squirmed in their chairs as she outlined new questions to explore, anxious about what that might mean for their workloads.

A marketer, who had floated in and out all day, once again advocated for a tactic she thought was brilliant. That conversation loop made the scientists crazy because the product concept was technically unfeasible. Trying to find harmony, the consumer insights director pointed out they had lots of data to help them decide the best path forward.

In the final hour of this all-day meeting, the discussion became divisive and tense—even though, in earlier work sessions, the team had aligned on success factors and key insights. Plus, they all agreed on one thing: the new product line that launched two years earlier had cannibalized the crown jewel of the company. But they were polarized on how to solve it. In the closing minutes of the meeting, an influential member of the team sniped, "We don't need more data; we just need to tell a story." Although he spoke a truth that others recognized—they didn't need more data or analysis—his comment made everyone feel awkward and confused.

The leader's cell phone buzzed, and she rushed out of the room to respond to another urgent situation. Everyone started to pack up and say goodbye to me. I found this an unsettling way for the day to end. I had no idea how I was going to pull this strategy together and help the team align.

(To be continued . . .)

Let's "Talk about the Weather"

As facilitators and project leaders, we've witnessed this team dynamic many times. The characters, roles, team dynamics, industries, and business challenges vary, but deciding when to stop analyzing and how to frame up the data already gathered is a common roadblock during the collaborative development of a strategy. Then, inevitably, someone volleys the question "So what's the story?" as if that's the magic answer.

These situations remind us of the scene in *Groundhog Day* when Bill Murray's character is greeted by the owner of the bed-and-breakfast with a polite question about the weather. When she looks baffled by his arrogant delivery of a detailed summary of the day's forecast, he snarks, "Do you really want to talk about the weather or just chitchat?" She admits, "Chitchat."

The challenge "So what's the story?" in business meetings sometimes reflects a team member's sincere concern that the strategy lacks cohesion and meaning. Often, it signals an underhanded criticism or an attempt to be clever and gain the upper hand. Regardless of where this comment is coming from, the challenge has a ring of truth: narrative techniques can help a team transform a pile of data into a compelling strategy.

Stakeholders need to see how the proposed ideas or concepts link back to broader business objectives before they'll give it a green light and funding. Story-based thinking at this critical juncture can help innovation leaders distill the leading ideas and possibilities into a cohesive strategy that shows how the proposed innovation will deliver business results (e.g., drive growth, generate profit, and increase loyalty). The strategy might include a broad set of initiatives along with specific product development plans. This chapter introduces a story-based tool for developing a strategic framework: the strategic arc. It also delves into how stories can help innovation leaders enlist support and mitigate resistance from stakeholders.

This chapter and the next focus on the top side of our model: gaining stakeholder support and alignment. These two chapters are complementary: chapter 6 applies a simple story structure to *craft* a strategy, while chapter 7 delves into narrative tools that can strengthen the *delivery* of strategy presentations and pitches.

The Strategic Arc

In *Made to Stick*, Chip Heath and Dan Heath, brothers and best-selling coauthors, argue that stories make ideas "sticky" and get people to act. They validate this assertion through a number of real-life business situations in which stories inspire action among employees, consumers, technicians, and executives. We go one step further by providing a framework for crafting strategies using a story structure: the strategic arc, a tool to align strategic and narrative elements.

Spinning a great tale is no substitute for the analytical and creative processes involved in innovation, but a great idea packaged in a compelling story has a better chance of advancing in the pipeline. The strategic arc plots a business analysis or strategy using the narrative arc for the purpose of inspiring stakeholders to take action (e.g., sponsor, endorse, or provide resources). When building a strategic arc, only include data that helps build tension, illuminates the pivotal insight, and fleshes out the strategies. Then land with a call to action. Put any other data in the backup materials—it's likely that 60 to 80 percent of what you gathered during discovery won't be important in telling the story.

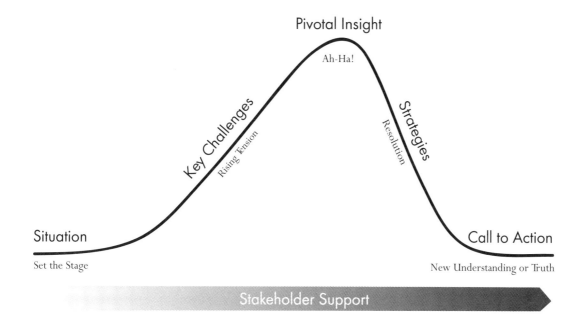

Situation

Strategic presentations typically start with a succinct statement of the nature of the problem or business challenge. Think of this as your opportunity to set the stage—to provide the backdrop and spotlight the core issue at hand. Your understanding of the situation might have evolved from where you started before the deep dive, so revisit your original assumptions. Distill the issue down to a *single* concept by peeling away tangents and secondary insights. Then find a concise and compelling way to express it.

Consider how you might grab your audience's attention while conveying essential background. For example, shake up current assumptions or norms with a surprising insight or shocking statistic. A consumer or user story might pull at heartstrings and reveal the challenge. Create a sense of intrigue by foreshadowing what's to come or portray the strategy as a mystery to solve. Pique your audience's curiosity to keep them listening.

Key Challenges

Projects generally have several inherent tensions that need to be addressed. During the discovery (exploration and clarification) phase of a project, many challenges can surface. Villains in the form of competitors, regulators, advocates, or consumers might introduce conflict. Technical limitations, competing priorities, deadlines, demanding customers, and internal resisters pose challenges to innovation. It's not uncommon for teams to get overwhelmed by all the problems that surface during a deep dive into new territory.

Identify and examine the range of tensions that might affect a project's success or failure. Then focus on one tension to serve as the backbone of the pitch. Prioritize the most relevant and compelling challenge—the one that pulls the strategy together. If they're vital, additional challenges can be addressed later as secondary considerations (e.g., constraints, guardrails, enablers, or assumptions).

Pivotal Insight

Select a singular insight that "cracks the code" of the problem and illuminates the path(s) forward. A pivotal insight isn't easy to discover, but in the end, it should be simply stated. Some people (as the Don Draper character depicts in *Mad Men)* are gifted at distilling divergent inputs into the essence of the challenge, and they make it look easy. That said, everyone can learn the skills to find the pivotal insight.

The big aha moment might elude you, but it's probably lingering somewhere in the insights you've compiled. Maybe it's something that surprised you during discovery, or perhaps it's been a nagging or recurring thought. You (and others) might be avoiding it because it's an uncomfortable or troubling truth.

You may need to iterate back and forth between determining the most critical challenge or tension and the pivotal insight. Try framing up the strategic pillars that logically flow from it to test if it's the right insight. If you end up on a flawed path forward, you probably need to back up and do some more discovery work to nail down the pivotal insight.

Once the pivotal insight is clear, express it in ten words or less (fewer than seven is better). Set it apart on a separate slide or visual aid. Punctuate it with a simple graphic or story to evoke emotion and imprint a memory. When you pitch the strategy, emphasize the pivotal insight by pausing for a moment to let the aha settle into the listeners' consciousness.

Key Strategies

Illustrate the path forward through the key strategies that resolve the challenge. It might help to clarify how the overarching strategies will chart a new course that resolves the challenge. It can be helpful to frame the strategy through a graphic (e.g., pillars, Venn diagram, windows, or pathways). Narrow the number of strategic paths to less than four—if you come up with eight, you're being too lofty or too granular.

At the strategic-framing stage, tactical details often distract stakeholders, causing them to dwell on unimportant minutiae and stealing focus from the main points. Only add action-planning details if the organization's culture dictates it. Be careful not to confuse tactics (the *how*) with strategies (the *what*). If your team members can't support the pitch without including tactical considerations, put these details in the backup or flag them as guardrails or considerations. Keep the pitch uncluttered so stakeholders' attention stays focused on the overall narrative and main points.

Unlock the Insight: Forward-Backward-Pivot

Just like parallel parking, you'll know you have the right pivot point if everything lines up after the pivot. You might have to inch forward and backward until you get correctly positioned, and you may need to pull out and start over. But when your car lines up with the curb and is equidistant from the cars in front and behind, you know you chose the right pivot point.

If the strategy fails to hold together, chances are you haven't accurately identified the key challenges and pivotal insight. Take the time to rewind and go over the previous steps. You'll be more seasoned the second, third, and fourth times, so don't dismiss this strategic backtracking as wasted time.

Those who have a bias for closure need to be patient during the back-and-forth steps of unlocking the pivotal insight. And those who love data need to be selective and let go of the details. A combination of individual reflection and collaborative dialogue will help tease out the pivotal insight. Use free-flowing tools—a whiteboard or an old-fashioned pencil, eraser, and scratch paper. Get comfortable with erasing and rewinding. Create, critique, and re-create. The pivotal insight will become clear. Sometimes the pivotal insight is glaringly obvious but the team members can't see it. In that case, the objective perspective of an outsider might be useful in reflecting it back to them.

Call to Action

Wrap up the pitch with a clear articulation of what will be different if the organization supports the change you propose. Consider what you need your stakeholders to do to advance the opportunity. Are you asking for alignment, approval, sponsorship, or resources? Land your story on a new understanding or truth that underpins the call to action. If you leave your stakeholders imagining future possibilities and intrigued to learn more, you'll have a better chance of getting approval to keep exploring . . . and, potentially, to execute.

"What's the Story?" Part 2

With the team misaligned on the strategic direction and only one week remaining to create the pitch, my head was spinning as I headed to the airport. Somewhere over the Rocky Mountains, I started to see a path forward for the team . . . and me. (I was anxious to close out this client engagement and move on to other commitments.)

I wrapped my brain around a few key takeaways. First, the team agreed on one pivotal insight: the new brand needed a differentiated positioning to capture new consumers and drive growth. If that challenge could be solved, the opportunities for the portfolio pipeline were plentiful and viable. The consumer insights director was right: they had data to support this decision. There was no time to process more data—I had to steer my client away from the idea that the answer could be found in new analyses. As a passionate believer in the power of stories, I knew there was some truth to the meeting's final snarky remark that we really needed to tell the story. Sure, that guy's motivation in the moment was more about voicing his frustrations over the team's lack of focus after spending so much time to clarify. But still, he had a point.

Back in my office the next day, I created the first version of the strategic arc. By framing the company's strategic process using a narrative arc, I illustrated for my client how we might pull together a unified strategy that (1) her team could support and (2) would lead the company in a bold new direction. She bought it! She especially loved how the "pivotal insight" unlocked the path forward. I created the pitch using a simple story structure to organize the immersion data and insights. Data or insights that didn't fit the strategic arc were moved to the backup. The team aligned on the draft pitch two days later. The executive team supported the approach, and I was hired back three months later to help the team develop a product pipeline to meet the needs of the new consumer segment they decided to target.

Constructing a Strategic Arc

The accompanying illustration sketches how the strategic arc was applied to the challenge in this story, in which the team was grappling with several challenges:

- The target market was unclear
- The product offering was "watered down" to appeal to the company's core consumer but these diluted benefits didn't deliver on new consumers' needs and wants
- The sales force didn't know or understand the new consumers or how the product offering worked in their lives

These were important problems to solve, but they were secondary to the positioning challenge. Teasing out these priorities was enabled by the strategic arc, which pivots on a singular insight that illuminates the path forward.

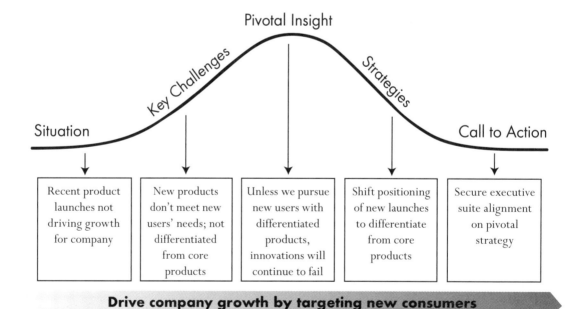

Using Stories in Stakeholder Engagement

Stakeholders include individuals, groups, or organizations that have an interest in the project and can mobilize resources to affect its outcome in some way. As Jean learned in her story "But He Hates Me" (at the top of chapter 1), stakeholders can help an initiative succeed or undermine its execution—in some cases, an adversarial stakeholder can stop it dead in its tracks.

If you haven't already engaged key stakeholders across the organization when a project progresses into development and implementation, take time to identify and understand the stakeholders who are likely to assist and those who might resist the initiative. Be deliberate and systematic in your outreach to key stakeholders. You could employ a stakeholder mapping tool to help you identify, evaluate, and prioritize everyone who can influence the initiative. Stakeholder maps assist with the development of an effective stakeholder communication and engagement strategy.

We recommend you also consider the stories that play out in your stakeholders' worlds and how these narratives might affect their response to your proposal. Anticipate how the execution of your plan might add tension and stress to their operations. Considering these stories will help you gain empathy for the people you need to influence and inspire them to consider your proposal in a more positive light.

Who Might Be Resisters and Assisters?

Whether you prefer to approach stakeholder management intuitively or analytically, it's helpful to consider who is likely to support and who might resist. Their assistance or resistance might come from the role they play, their personality, or both. Take some time to identify all the people you need to bring on board for the project to be successfully executed. As you compile a list of assisters and resisters, consider the roles key stakeholders play.

Leaders Who Influence the Final Decision

Managers up the line in your function are obvious, but don't forget about cross-functional leaders who sit on leadership teams and control resources you might need. These senior leaders generally don't tolerate minutiae, so don't bog them down with tactical details. They need to see how your proposal can bring value to the organization and what's in it for them. Vision and user stories—alongside concepts and prototypes that illustrate how this initiative can bring business results—are likely to get them excited.

Employees and Functions Affected by the Change

The leaders of functions and teams whose work will be changed as a result of the innovation may oppose your proposal unless you give them a reason to believe the innovation can also benefit their teams—or serve a higher purpose for the company. What stories might help them see your initiative in that light?

Leaders Who Provide Key Resources

The functional leaders and their day-to-day managers who oversee the human resources needed to execute the project provide the lubrication for smooth execution. People rally around a higher purpose, so vision and user stories might help to energize them. Stories that show you understand how your proposal will affect their teams' work will help leaders see you're concerned with more than just advancing your own agenda.

These stakeholders usually appreciate the opportunity to have input on the project's scope and timeline. Also, they often seek to clarify roles before they agree to take on more work.

Members of the Execution Team

The people who do the work to execute the project are critical. During development and implementation, new players might join the team. Chapter 5 explores a range of story techniques to engage and guide the work of execution teams. If you discover key members of the execution team are resisting, take some time to gain empathy for their point of view. As you hear their stories, think about how to mitigate the difficulties they anticipate. Then share a story that paints a brighter vision for how this innovation would add value to their lives.

Interested Parties

Consider including key subject matter experts and go-to influencers in your outreach efforts. Influencers are those people others turn to while forming opinions about risks and opportunities; they don't always have functional authority. Interested parties might be legal and regulatory experts, or technical contributors. In his book *The Tipping Point*, popular author and journalist Malcolm Gladwell characterizes these information brokers as the "mavens." Many organizations also have go-to people who've built an internal reputation for spotting and advancing innovation.

Stakeholder Story Analysis

As you prepare for stakeholder meetings, think about your proposal from their point of view. Casual one-on-one conversations with key stakeholders ahead of larger group meetings are invaluable. Go into these conversations with the goal of understanding and gaining empathy for their perspective. Don't plow over their concerns. Use the story listening skills we share in chapter 3 and story interview guide in appendix C to gather understanding and insights. Stakeholders fall into two categories—assisters and resisters—and it's vital to identify which category each stakeholder occupies and respond accordingly.

Assisters are positively disposed to your initiative and are easier to enlist, but don't ignore the reality that no one likes to be blindsided or bulldozed. Don't assume you have their support. Do your homework, and take time to brief them on the project to build credibility and trust.

Resisters are more challenging. Often their resistance stems from a perceived or real threat presented by your initiative. Going back to the story, "But He Hates Me" at the beginning of chapter 1, Cliff believed Jean's new programming initiatives disrupted his operations and made more work for him. Innovation often disrupts the status quo—anticipate how your initiative might impact another person's work. Sometimes resistance is simply a function of the stakeholder's personality or work style. When you face both, winning over resisters takes savvy and skills in stakeholder management.

Before telling your story, take time to learn their story. We're sharing some thought starters about what stories might play out in various forms of resistance, but don't assume you know what's going on in their world. Show genuine concern and respect for the roles they play, then listen . . . listen . . . listen. Once you have some insights, archetypes and universal plots might help you make sense of what you hear. Then select a story that taps into their motives and addresses the source of resistance. We like to use a Stakeholder Story Analysis framework to identify the potential concerns of the people who might resist the innovation.

Incorporating Stories into Stakeholder Analysis

Source of Resistance	What Is Their Story?	Story to Overcome Resistance
Technical Feasibility and efficacy Scientific credibility Regulatory constraints	Technical experts are concerned about the feasibility and integrity of the solution.	"The Technical Team Saved the Day" Shine a light on what technical experts do to show that you value what they bring. Help other members of the team see them as heroes rather than naysayers.
Functional Turf wars Competition for resources Conflict between roles and accountability Personality and power clashes	Stakeholders want to protect their turf and people. Differing priorities between functions create inherent tensions.	"When Opportunity Was Disguised as Loss" Tell a story about an experience when at first you thought you'd gotten the short end of a deal, but, in the long run it turned out to be the best outcome. Maybe you were rewarded later or became more resilient.
Cultural Institutional norms Status quo Sacred cows	Stakeholders fear retribution if they step outside accepted norms and approaches.	"Challenger O-Ring Failure" The team at NASA operated in a culture where everyone "went along to get along," so those who saw flaws in the O-ring design were reluctant to speak up, with horrifically fatal results. Every team needs critical thinkers. High-performing teams cultivate a safe climate to speak up.
Political Power struggles Natural order disrupted	Stakeholders are competing for power and dominance in the organization. Your project may be a pawn in a larger battle.	"Speaking Truth to Power" or "The Impossible Odds" David-versus-Goliath or Atticus Finch stories won't break up power struggles that are beyond your control, but they cast the little person as a hero and inspire everyday acts of bravery.

Closing Thoughts

By using a story structure to frame a strategy, you can create pitches that have more dramatic effect. You can modify the strategic arc with the strategic elements or pitch structure commonly used in your organization.

The strategic arc creates an intriguing sequence and flow to a pitch. It also helps in sorting through which supporting material is relevant. Include data, insights, and information that supports the story. Discipline yourself to eliminate extraneous details that don't help tell the story. Just because immersion details were important to your learning journey, stakeholders don't need that level of detail. Be prepared to leave 80 percent of immersion material in your files and archives. If you think someone might ask you a detailed question and you want to refer to it just in case, put it in a backup section or print a copy for your reference.

A strategy hinges on nailing the pivotal insight. Just like parallel parking, you'll know you have the right pivot point if everything lines up after the pivot. You might need to iterate back and forth between the key challenges, pivotal insight, and the strategies.

The Art of Explanation by Lee LeFever, a renowned expert in creating user-friendly manuals and videos for high-tech products, provides clever and practical ways to make complex topics simple and easy to understand. Insights professionals and technical experts should keep a copy on their desks. The well-known business books *Made to Stick* and *Switch* by Chip Heath and Dan Heath and *Tipping Point* by Malcolm Gladwell touch on how stories can enable strategic leadership. A number of other business storytelling books—such as *StoryBranding* by Jim Signorelli, *Putting Stories to Work* by Shawn Callahan, and *Business Storytelling for Dummies* by Karen Dietz and Lori L. Silverman—offer useful insights and methods to blend stories into stakeholder communications.

Coming up with winning ideas that pass consumer tests is no small undertaking, but many winning ideas never make it to the market because they get killed by stakeholders. Skilled innovation leaders know how to gain the support of stakeholders who approve the project and allocate resources. Story listening and storytelling can help to break down resistance and engender support.

> *In the middle of difficulty lies opportunity.*
> —ALBERT EINSTEIN

7

Pitches, Presentations, and Elevator Speeches

How to persuade and influence with stories

"Paper or Plastic?"
By Jean Storlie

Sitting in the back of the ballroom, I was getting ready to speak at a nutrition professional conference, only half listening to the opening remarks of a keynote speech about working with older adults. When the speaker started by telling a story about taking her eighty-six-year-old father to the grocery store, my head sprang out of my notes. Here's how I recall her story:

> When we entered the supermarket, I let Dad take his own cart and wander the aisles because he was persnickety about his independence. After finishing my shopping, I got into the checkout line behind him and noticed that he was flustered and upset. I asked, "Dad, what's wrong?" He pointed to the clerk. "Did you hear what she said? She just told me to 'Pay up, bastard.'" Then it dawned on me: "No, no, Dad! She was asking if you want paper or plastic."

I heard this speaker several years ago, and I wish I could remember her name now. Needless to say, her story has stuck with me. It vividly portrays the communication challenges associated with hearing loss. She also used other themes from the story to underscore key points of her talk. Through the "Paper or Plastic?" episode, she distilled theories and research into simple and memorable principles.

Years later, I still remember her key messages—even though the topic isn't relevant to my work—because of her effective use of this simple, amusing story. She told a great tale and also modeled how to weave a story into a professional presentation.

Let Me Tell You a Story . . .

Nothing is worse than sitting in an audience as a speaker begins with "I'm going tell you a story," then rambles through a lengthy, unfocused anecdote. But as "Paper or Plastic?" illustrates, a strong opening story can set a positive tone, capture the audience's attention, and establish credibility. Likewise, stories sprinkled throughout a presentation emphasize key messages, explain complicated concepts, and persuade others to take action.

Building on the previous chapter, which introduced a simple story structure to craft a strategic presentation, this chapter delves into narrative tools to strengthen the *delivery* of a pitch or presentation. Well-chosen and well-told stories enchant audiences, leaving a lasting and moving impression that changes how the listener thinks and feels. Skilled speakers make it seem effortless, but chances are they put a lot of thought into selecting the story and practicing their delivery.

Weaving Stories into Pitches and Presentations

An appropriate, well-delivered story can punctuate a presentation and leave the audience reflecting on your messages long after they leave the room. But long-winded or irrelevant jokes and stories often detract from a speaker's credibility and turn off audiences.

To avoid derailing your message, think carefully about the purpose the story will serve in the presentation and find a suitable story. It might help to brainstorm stories related to the topic and then tease out what role the story will play. Or you might prefer to clarify the intent of an opening story before seeking out a story that fits. It's often a circular process.

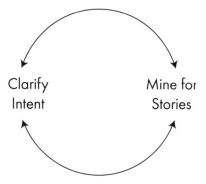

Clarify the Intent of the Story

Stories reinforce the content of a presentation by strengthening an argument, explaining a nuanced situation, building empathy, or tapping into imagination. They also help manage the group dynamics required when pitching to stakeholders: building trust, addressing conflict, and gaining alignment. Many stories do both.

Brainstorm all the possibilities for how a story might be used in your pitch. Then mine for stories. If you find one that might work, highlight all the linkages, then go back to your outline to see how to thread the story throughout the speech. Sketching a mind map might help you explore possibilities and converge on the strategic intent of a story.

While clarifying the strategic intent, also consider the best vehicle for delivery. Should you tell it yourself or play an audio or video clip? A brief snippet from consumer interactions, a movie, or a YouTube post might reveal the story better than you can. You also may want to have a condensed version of the story prepared in the event your time gets trimmed at the last minute.

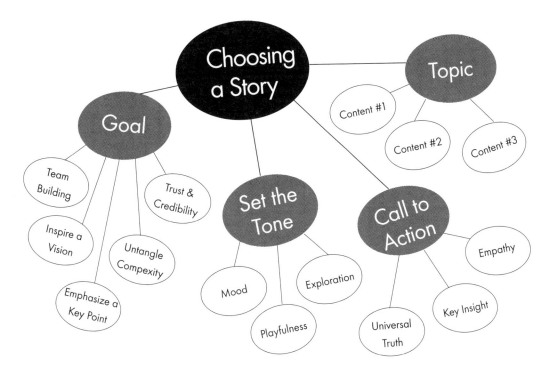

Mine for Stories

Once in a blue moon, a story might find you . . . and you know instantly that it's perfectly suited for the situation. But usually you have to go searching for them. There are many places to find stories, so don't be discouraged if the muse doesn't make a timely visit with inspiration. Stories beget stories, so start finding stories and let your mind wander. To get started, here are some sources to consider:

Personal Stories

Everyone's life contains a treasure trove of experiences that can be turned into stories. Take a walk down memory lane for stories from your work and personal life that link to the topic of your presentation. The Mining for Story Gems worksheet in the online tool kit includes story prompts to explore stories from work and life.

Fables and Fairytales

Browse through children's books and fables. Explore folklore from different cultures to bring new stories into your world. *The Power of Metaphor* by Michael Berman and David Brown includes a compilation of parables and folktales from around the world that may add inspiration to your pitch.

Company or Organization Stories

Look within your organization for relevant stories. Employee or workplace stories reveal a human side of business topics. Brand or consumer stories show how real people's struggles might be solved with a brand promise or benefit. If you work in health care, patient stories might reveal the emotional side of a medical event. User and customer experiences uncover design flaws and successes.

Books and Movies

Many popular books and movies are based on universal plots with widely applicable themes. It might be hard to recap an entire book or movie when opening a speech, but a representative clip or passage could meet your needs. Stick to popular or classic works, because an excerpt from an obscure story might lack context and fail to connect with the audience.

Pop Culture

You might be able to connect your topic to an inspiring current event. Skim the news, YouTube, and Google. Steer clear of polarizing topics to avoid alienating anyone in your audience. Likewise, be cautious of current events that fire up some people but leave others flat (e.g., sports or celebrity gossip). Stories that are inclusive and convey a universal message will be most effective.

Jokes

Many speakers open with a joke, which can be an effective way to break the ice and relax an audience. Funny stories, like jokes, start a speech on an entertaining note. Avoid self-deprecating humor, which can unintentionally undermine your credibility. Similarly, jokes at others' expense and put-downs alienate your audience. In a professional setting, *never* cross the line with off-color humor.

Tips for Using Audio and Video Clips

If you use technology, make sure it works perfectly. Practice how to segue to the audio or video clip then seamlessly grab your audience's attention back. You probably have at most one to three minutes to set up the clip, show it, and link it to your topic. Make sure you don't lose your audience during the transitions or let the story overpower your presentation. Connect the story's deeper meaning to your topic.

Where to Use Stories in the Pitch

You can include a story anywhere along the strategic arc, but don't overdo it. Too many stories, especially if they're long and complicated can take the focus off the strategy and meeting objectives. An overabundance of stories can leave the impression that you're flaky or scattered.

Be strategic in deciding where a story will fit best in the pitch. Use one story for a brief presentation, maybe two if you have an hour or longer. Keep practicing the art of telling stories in fifteen seconds to one minute. (Refer to chapter 1 for tips and tools about how to craft business stories.)

Let's consider how stories might be used in different parts of a pitch: opening, rising tension, pivotal insight, or closure. Also refer to the accompanying table for ideas on how to design breakout activities to get participants involved in telling stories during a presentation. If you want to sprinkle inspirational quotes into your presentation, appendix E highlights evocative quotes from famous leaders (plus others that inspire us).

Opening

As Will Rogers said, "You never have a second chance to make a first impression." "Paper or Plastic?" illustrates how a story can accomplish many goals for opening remarks. First, the story was brief, which is critical for an opening story when the audience is still deciding whether to listen or tune out. It grabbed attention—even pulled me out of deep concentration. The speaker's use of humor relaxed the audience and created a human connection. Her personal story provided context and background for the topic and revealed key insights. In addition, she wove the story into the body of the presentation.

If you find a story that accomplishes all those goals and you practice telling it well, your speech will make a positive first impression. Practice over and over again until the words flow naturally—with emotional emphasis at the right moments. When the first words out of your mouth are rehearsed, the rest will come naturally.

Rising Tension

Use a story to develop the tension and draw out empathy for the human angle of the situation. A consumer, user, employee, or leadership story might illuminate a challenge and the dilemma it represents. You could also develop the plot of an opening story to build intrigue and suspense. Remember that a story involves a character struggling and this is the part of the story that reveals who the character is and what he or she is facing.

If you're pitching a new product idea, a consumer or user narrative could fit well in the rising tension part of your pitch. If you're advocating for an organization or culture change, leadership or employee stories could be powerful. A founder or values story can help an organization return to its roots to get back on course.

Seek a representative story that gets to the heart of the tension and sheds light on the pivotal insight.

Pivotal Insight

The most dramatic element of a strategy—the pivotal insight—might be revealed through a story. Rather than inserting a story detour before you reveal the pivotal insight, time the story to sync with the peak of your strategic arc. Business audiences get annoyed with convoluted communications—these settings are not the place for epic tales with complex subplots.

Closure

Like the punchline of a joke, ending a pitch with a story pulls together all the threads of the pitch and leaves the listener pondering key insights. The right closing story can leave stakeholders reflecting on the "So what?" as well as the *what* of your pitch.

Story Breakout Exercises

If you have	Try these activities	Instructions	Examples
1–3 minutes	Interactively reading a story aloud	Go around the room and take turns reading passages from the story.	• Cookie Thief • Dr. Seuss book • Children's book
3–5 minutes	Pair and Share	Have participants grab a partner and share an anecdote or brief story about the topic with each other.	• Your first car • Your best boss • A close call • Feedback you'll never forget • A mistake you learned from
10–15 minutes	Six-Word Story Spin Around	Give everyone a little time to reflect quietly about a story related to the topic, then find six words to tell their story. Rotate around to share the stories.	• Leadership value • A mentor • A time you felt like a fish out of water • Great customer service you received
10–20 minutes	Story Game	Refer to chapter 8 for ideas about how to use games.	• Rory's Story Cubes • MadLibs • Catch Phrase • Who What Where • Telestrations

Women's Bean Project

Tamra Ryan, CEO of Women's Bean Project, uses stories in many facets of her leadership of this social enterprise. Women's Bean Project employs chronically impoverished and unemployed women and helps them earn the job-readiness, interpersonal, and life skills to create a new future—for themselves, their families, our community, and our economy. Tamra speaks on the national stage about the Women's Bean Project and, more broadly, how social enterprise can achieve profitable business goals along with social impact. She conveys the women's change stories in her formal and informal communications with employees, investors, donors, and volunteers. These stories also inspire lifestyle change in the women themselves. In one of her keynote addresses, Tamra opened with this true story about one of their clients, Charlotte.

"Charlotte Was Born an Addict"

Charlotte's mother got her hooked on heroin in utero. Charlotte spent the first eight years of her life on methadone, a nonaddictive heroin replacement, only to get hooked again at ten when her uncle shot her up with cocaine in his first step to controlling and abusing her. She never told anyone in order to protect her siblings and cousins.

Into her late twenties Charlotte was an addict. Eventually, her addiction led to a number of run-ins with the criminal justice system, earning her a three-year sentence in a halfway house. That's where she was living when we hired her last year. Charlotte was almost thirty years old when she became one of my coworkers. At that point she'd been clean and sober for eighteen months—the longest period of her life.

I work at a place called Women's Bean Project, where we believe all women have the power to transform their lives through employment. So we hire women who've been chronically unemployed and teach them to work by creating nourishing products. They learn to stand tall, find their purpose, and end the cycle of poverty. Ultimately, we know that when you change a woman's life, you change her family's life.

We hire women convicted of felonies—often several—and with long histories of addiction. They haven't held a job longer than a year in their lifetime. Their average age is thirty-eight. One might say we hire the worst workers rather than the best.

We make a line of gourmet food mixes that started with bean soup, which was the genesis of our name. Our products are distributed in nearly one thousand stores across the country and online through some of the nation's largest retailers. But the products are just a part of our story. To truly understand what we do, you have to understand who we hire.

We hire women who need to learn workplace norms like coming to work every day and on time, taking direction, and paying attention to detail. We hire women who need to learn life skills like problem solving, budgeting, planning, and organizing. After six to nine months they graduate and move to entry-level jobs in the community where they can advance, prosper, and (too often) feel valued for the first time in their lives.

Such is the case with Charlotte, a short Latina who hides her femininity beneath her baggy clothes and a buzz cut. She's still young—just barely thirty. At the Bean Project Charlotte learned the skills you need to have a job.

But she said the most important thing she gained at Women's Bean Project was feeling that someone finally cared about her. All she ever wanted, she said, is to be cared for.

And that's what we do at Women's Bean Project. We care. We create a safe and accepting work environment where women like Charlotte can move beyond their past and begin to focus on their future.

Social enterprises like ours use the entrepreneurial skills and talents of the team to advance their missions. That requires doing some things differently than a business without a social mission.

First, we must exhibit and exercise strong empathy. Second, we have to serve in the roles of mentors and coaches to drive successful outcomes. And we have to create a safe, accepting, and nurturing work environment.

All of this is built into our business model.

—Tamra Ryan

In her book, *The Third Law*, Tamra shares other amazing stories of these women's dramatic life transformations. Through their stories, she reveals how working with these women transformed her worldview. As she explores how chronically unemployed and impoverished women change their lives, Tamra elucidates the many societal forces that push back on them. Over time she realized that what it takes for women to change their lives is other people believing in them.

Elevator Speeches

"I didn't have time to write a short letter, so I wrote a long one instead" (famous quote attributed to Cicero, Pascal, Mark Twain, and Winston Churchill). Networking receptions, icebreakers, job interviews, and random encounters with important people present opportunities to make a positive impression in a brief interaction. Telling a long-winded, rambling, or pointless story is a sure way to blow it, but that doesn't mean storytelling is off-limits in these situations. You just need to have a few relevant stories top of mind and be able to share one in twenty to thirty seconds—or the amount of time it takes to ride up or down one floor on an elevator. A little effort and time to prepare a collection stories for these brief encounters can keep you from leaving a lame impression or—even worse—embarrassing yourself.

Six Leadership Stories . . . Told in Six Words

Influence stories that you've curated and developed can enhance your leadership impact in networking, job interviews, and other professional interactions. Taking time to prepare a collection of stories that reveal who you are as a leader and what you stand for can pay off over and over again. After some reflection, you'll probably discover that certain moments of your life defined your character and leadership style. We encourage you to curate and develop these as go-to stories for career-building situations.

Annette Simmons is a pioneer of business storytelling and the author of several books on the topic. In her first book, *The Story Factor*, she introduced a widely used model: six stories to persuade and influence. She describes how six core stories establish rapport, credibility, and trust—which can help you lead and persuade others. Her six-story framework might help you identify some of your core leadership stories.

- "Who I Am" stories
- "Why I'm Here" stories
- "Vision" stories
- "Teaching" stories
- "Values in Action" stories
- "I Know What You're Thinking" stories

Once you've identified your go-to stories, we recommend you develop them using the "Develop Plot and Meaning" process we introduced in chapter 1. Practice telling the story in less than three minutes. Then cut it to less than two minutes, then less than one.

When your story is clear and concise, take the Hemingway challenge: find a way to tell these stories in six words or less. The six-word limit imposes a constraint that yields a sense of mystery and often piques curiosity. Experience tells us it's a wonderful way to spark dialogue and inspire the other person to ask you questions about the story. Use the six-word version in networking conversations, during job interviews, or if you land in an elevator with a key stakeholder or someone you'd like to influence. Then, as time permits, you can share your longer versions if the listener shows interest.

Here are few of Jean's six-word stories:

- Automatic Out! Storlie's Up!
- A Writing Career despite C+ English
- Klutzy, Ridiculed Kid Became Fitness Professional
- 1968 Ford Galaxy: Lessons on Mentoring
- Rescued While Skating on Thin Ice
- My Opportunity Disguised as Loss

Here are few of Mimi's six-word stories:

- My Fourteen Ideas Fell Flat
- The "Broccoli Girl" Finds Her Tribe
- Play the Twos. And a Twenty-Four.
- We Are Not Tight-Pants People
- Went Back. Was Same. I Changed.
- Year of Meats on East Campus

Advocacy Stories

Whether you're advancing a project or a cause, collect brief stories that reveal compelling insights ready for stakeholder conversations. You never know when you might step on an elevator with a key decision-maker and have a chance to influence. Consider stories that represent a new perspective about consumers or users. Stories that get you excited and passionate are good choices because your natural enthusiasm will spill into storytelling and reveal a bit about yourself at the same time. Lastly, stories that touch on a universal truth touch heartstrings and have broad appeal.

For example, Jean's former boss (a company vice president) was engaged in a budget-cutting debate with her peers. When someone suggested that her department could make up the shortfall, she replied, "We have no funds to cut: our budget is smaller than Mother Teresa's wardrobe." While not a full-blown story, her metaphorical reference to saintly poverty shut down further suggestions of raiding her budget.

Have your advocacy stories ready to insert into conversations and brief encounters. You can use the six-word challenge to tell the stories, or simply sketch out fifteen- to twenty-second versions of them.

How to Tell a Good Story

Throw yourself into a story by practicing and experimenting with not only the words but also your delivery of the words. In preparing for her first storytelling workshop, Jean wrote all her stories out ahead of time, but she didn't practice telling them. Even though she knew them by heart, her delivery flopped miserably because the stories came off as phony and forced. A participant sat her down afterward and delivered the best feedback she ever received: tell your stories; don't recite them. From that day forward, every time Jean gets ready for a presentation, she practices the stories out loud—even if she's telling a story that she's told a hundred times before.

Choose Perspective and Plot

Consider whether you'll be the narrator or a character in the story and choose a perspective. For example, you may play the omnipotent narrator who has access to all the thoughts and feeling of all characters in the story. Or maybe you'll tell it from the first-person perspective—as the main character who doesn't know what others are thinking and feeling unless they tell you. Revisit the chapter 5 discussion about selecting the perspective or point of view to help you make this decision. Sketch out the plot—or backbone—of your story. If you get the plot right, you're halfway to a good story. The storytelling fundamentals covered in chapter 1 apply to oral storytelling, so get familiar with those techniques.

Practice Out Loud

Oral storytelling, like any skill, develops with practice. Just like the first time you got on a bicycle, you may feel a little wobbly at first. But through practice and experimentation, you'll find a style that works for you. We found practical advice for developing oral storytelling skills from Jack Maguire, who is an early advocate of introducing time-tested storytelling methods to transform interpersonal communications. In his book *The Power of Personal Storytelling*, Maguire describes a technique he calls "Out Loud and Proud." Here's a brief summary:

- Find a place where you feel safe to talk out loud to yourself. Many people like to roam around rather than sit.
- Ponder the story idea for a few minutes in solitude. Break it down into the scenes that reveal the narrative arc. Spend time imagining salient details (sights, sounds, smells, tastes, and touches) that your listener might want to hear.
- While still in this safe place, start talking out loud. Let your story tumble out.
- When you get stuck, pause and reflect on what you've said already and what comes next. Remember that you're alone and safe—so feel free to rewind, redirect, and reword.
- End your practice when you think you have it right. Capture notes and audio recordings to help you pick up again later. Walk away and practice again later, picking up where you left off.

Practicing alone and out loud is the best way to get ready for a presentation. Once you're comfortable alone, try the story out in front of a peer, friend, or family member. Jean's colleague, Jenn, used to place stuffed animals around a room and pretend they were participants. She would have imaginary interactions with the animals to practice audience engagement techniques. Once you have a feel for your story, time yourself. Cut extraneous details and tighten up your delivery so your story fits within the allotted time. When you've said the story out loud enough times, it will roll off your lips.

Stories are like snowflakes. Not only is each story different, but so is every telling of the same story. Rather than memorizing a story, embrace the uniqueness of each telling.

Add Nonverbal Techniques

As you practice and refine your story, play around with gestures, facial expressions, and movements to add emphasis and dramatic flair. Is there a passage where you could act out what a character does (e.g., fling your hair, wipe off sweat, slam a door, gobble down food, chase after a bus) or imitate his or her voice? You might play two characters engaged in a dialogue by shifting your stance and changing your voice. Simple props (e.g., a hat, walking stick, coffee mug, or shopping bag) provide visual symbols that reveal a character's role or personality.

Use Your Voice as a Dramatic Tool

Pauses emphasize key moments in the story's action. Match your tone, pace, and volume to the mood you want to create. A slow, steady, calm voice creates a very different mood than a loud, booming, intimidating voice.

Closing Thoughts

Storytelling is buzzing in the business world, and we hear the term *story* tossed around loosely. People love to say they're going to tell a story, but then they don't. Conference speakers declare "Let me tell you a story," then string together a boring series of events or go off on a speculative tangent. Another phrase we often hear is "We're going to take our customer on our journey." These leaders don't consider whether or not the discovery and development journey is meaningful or how the journey could be turned into a story. This phrase becomes an excuse to tell a detailed saga without consideration of what the audience cares to hear.

We observe many health-care organizations run marketing campaigns with "patient stories." But health-care administrators make the mistake of thinking that if an actual person makes a statement about a real-life event, then it's a story. Health events provide a lot of grist to create a story, but typically these patient stories are nothing more than testimonials (e.g., "I'm so happy Dr. John delivered my baby."). Use the storytelling fundamentals introduced in chapter 1 to find, craft, and polish stories for your business communications.

It takes some planning and homework to effectively use a story in a pitch or presentation. Be strategic in selecting the story. Start by clarifying the role of a story in the pitch or presentation, then mine for stories to find one that fits. Your next decisions are where to insert the story and how you will share it. Will you use a video or audio clip or tell it yourself? Depending on the setting and size of the audience, you could turn the story sharing into an interactive activity. Refer back to chapter 4 for techniques to engage an audience in storytelling exercises. Chapter 5 explores ways to tell user stories.

Some people feel reluctant to tell stories, especially in work settings. They might feel nervous about getting started. We hear them say, "My wife is the storyteller. I just listen." You don't need to be the life of the party to become a good storyteller. Timid, soft-spoken people can tell compelling and moving stories that reflect their authentic and understated style. Other people resist because they're uncomfortable revealing who they are. But as Annette Simmons asserts, stories about "who you are" and "why you're here" actually build credibility and trust.

We hope you have fun playing around with stories in your presentations and find your authentic voice as a storyteller.

Always be a first-rate version of yourself rather than a second-rate version of someone else.
—Judy Garland

8

Facilitate with Stories

Stories create meaningful and memorable team events

"Your Mission, Should You Choose to Accept It..."
By Jean Storlie

The Mission Impossible theme music grabs the team's attention as a figure in a trench coat with an upturned collar and fedora pulled low slinks into the room and leaves a briefcase at the front of the room. A few minutes later, the project leader walks into the room and, after some furtive glances to the right and left, carefully opens the briefcase. A tape recording begins [narrator evokes the briefer's serious voice]:

> *Good morning, Mr. Leader. We face a serious situation that requires the Mission Impossible Innovation Team. We're losing out on our fair share of a $60-billion opportunity. Your mission, should you choose to accept it, is to seize a fair share of this growth opportunity for [brand]. But to do that you must define the consumer benefit territories. The territory teams will address different consumer segments and determine how this opportunity can beat back the competition.*
>
> *Each team has instructions and materials to help them complete the mission. They will work hard, but each team has the tools and expertise to contribute to the mission. As a team, they must: (1) understand their challenge, (2) prioritize and synthesize their ideas, (3) refine high-potential ideas into working concepts, and (4) build an opportunity map for their benefit territory.*
>
> *The territory teams will report back on how they cracked the code. Teams will detail how each territory can help the overall brand strategy. They will recommend short-, medium-, and long-term actions. Finally, they will provide a point of view on how to unify the territories under a common rallying cry.*

Mr. Leader, go out there with your Mission Impossible Innovation Team and infiltrate future growth opportunities and find the trophy that will create leadership for [brand].

As always, if you or any of your innovation operators are caught or killed, the Secretary will disavow any knowledge of your actions. Good luck, Mr. Leader."

[Recording self-destructs.]

Rally a Team around a Mission

Jean uses variations of this *Mission Impossible*–inspired skit in both team-building and innovation sessions. It's a type of story, but it's also an example of how a story-themed event might be designed. We think of this as a bonus chapter. It explores a range of ways stories can be used to design events that stand out from the ordinary. We decided to include this chapter, even though it's not a straight-up fit with the rest of the book, because we both have a passion for combining subtle and dramatic story elements into our session designs to create memorable and meaningful events.

Stories infused into team events build camaraderie and inspire team members to rally around shared goals. Iconic stories and events—for example, *Mission Impossible*, *Star Wars*, *The Wizard of Oz*, the Olympic Games, the World Cup, or fairy tales—provide a backdrop to inspire imagination and resolve tension in business meetings.

The *Mission Impossible* skit in the opening story was designed for an innovation session during a themed event. The team needed to work collaboratively in subgroups to accomplish a shared goal. In context, the *Mission Impossible* theme served a number of purposes:

- Broke the ice and created a laugh track
- Leveraged the theme to define the challenge
- Unified breakout teams around their mission
- Provided a forced connection for ideation
- Set the tone for a creative environment
- Encouraged healthy competition among team members

The mystery and intrigue evoked by *Mission Impossible* pairs well with innovation and strategic-planning sessions. But it could just as easily be used to inspire a team to rally around a shared goal, such as writing its annual objectives. Similarly, other story themes and techniques can help to unify and guide teams during collaboration. This chapter will explore various ways stories can be added to a facilitator's toolbox.

Create Memorable Team Experiences

The invocation "once upon a time" conjures childhood memories. Spice up team-building events, training workshops, celebrations, or innovation and strategic-planning sessions with stories to keep participants thinking about the meeting long after they leave the room. In his book, *The Accelerated Learning Handbook*, Dave Meier emphasizes the importance of designing sessions that engage the whole brain—its logical and intellectual capabilities, along with emotion and the subconscious—to engage participants quickly and deeply in learning and problem solving. Stories are one way to do that.

Stories create human connections. People relax and relate to one another differently after they share stories. It can be as simple as casually pairing people to share two- to three-minute stories, or something more structured and elaborate. Sprinkle stories and story-based activities throughout a session to energize and inspire a group. Or organize an entire event around a story, using characters and elements of the story to design collateral materials and activities.

Casual storytelling fosters teamwork and camaraderie. One of Jean's clients began the practice of starting every team meeting with a few minutes of open-ended story sharing. After a year, the leader observed a transformation in her team's culture: they began to trust each other more and were able to address tough issues with more openness and less tension. Consider how you might create a culture of storytelling to enhance regular team meetings, quarterly team-building events, and year-end celebrations.

Mission Impossible–Themed Innovation Event

The dramatic frame of the *Mission Impossible* franchise was used to evoke the mysterious and adventurous aspects of innovation. To bring some levity to an innovation working session, the day kicked off with a skit based on the movies' iconic opening scenes. The *Mission Impossible* formula began when the agent was briefed through a recording that self-destructed. The theme was used in designing the activities and meeting experience. As session inspiration, music and props helped capture attention and imagination.

In this case, a cross-functional team was tasked with developing a road map to generate growth by capitalizing on a large consumer trend. A twelve-member team had spent six weeks gathering data and insights about the market size, consumer, scientific evidence, and competition. After an ideation session, the team had identified and refined the high-potential ideas and sorted them into three opportunity areas (i.e., territories).

They were reconvening to assimilate all this work into a three-pronged strategy. Tension was high with different team members misaligned on tactical details, and the team needed to pitch the strategy to senior executives a week later. The *Mission Impossible* theme carried through to the breakout team assignments. Forming teams with defined roles and fostering competition between teams helped to dissipate some of the conflict.

Manage Group Dynamics

Have you ever been in a meeting where the elephant in the room—the unspoken but obvious conflict no one wants to acknowledge or discuss—is one dynamic while the agenda operates as a separate, disconnected conversation? When that happens, people leave the meeting confused, and speculation about "what's going on" drowns out productive follow-through efforts. A facilitator or leader can tell a story that acknowledges the "elephant" without naming it and, in so doing, dissipate tension.

For example, I watched a senior executive do this brilliantly. He dissipated conflict and anxiety around the rollout of a new budgeting prioritization model by talking about how they could move it forward in the context of a "first date." This metaphor piqued their interest. Anxiety melted into curiosity. He pantomimed, "On a first date, you say, 'What do you want to do?' 'I don't know. Whatever you want to do.' The awkward volley continues until someone says, 'Let's do [X].'" He reminded them that the new budget model would be uncomfortable but that they needed to put a stake in the ground so they could move forward. The tension evaporated, and the competing factions rolled up their sleeves and started to draft a budget.

Stories also help leaders and facilitators address other challenging group dynamics. In the *Mission Impossible* innovation event, the themed activity channeled the divisive dynamics that had been playing out with the team in prior sessions. A productive outlet for their competitive energy and a spirit of play helped them collaborate more harmoniously.

Every organization has internal struggles over competing priorities. Organizational units experience inherent tensions because they're accountable for different work. For example, sourcing might get frustrated with sales because they overpromise and then blame sourcing when the customer is unhappy with an outcome. Some of these tensions can be mitigated through the language of creative problem solving. Reframe critical thoughts into a new creative challenge by asking a question like "How might we?"

Another simple way to reduce tension is through carving out time for participants to share stories with each other. They start to see their colleagues as people rather than as someone who represents an opposing function in the organization. Stories foster personal connections—and personal connections help people find common ground.

Mitigating Common Clashes with Stories

Common Clashes	Stories You Might Hear	How to Mitigate
Marketing and R&D: competitive messaging versus technical feasibility.	"Marketing hyperbole distorts the science." "R&D has no imagination."	Showcase stories that cast the opposing teams in a positive light.

Share a story that helps others walk a mile in someone else's shoes.

Tell a story about how an underdog saved the day.

Have conflicting parties share a "Who I Am" or "Why I'm Here" story to build trust and respect for each other. |
R&D and operations: work in the lab versus reality in the plant.	"The new formula slows down production." "The plant always resists innovation."	
Legal says no.	"You never get a new idea past legal." "Legal loves to kill creativity."	
Sourcing and sales: pleasing the customer versus fulfilling promises.	"Sales overpromises, and sourcing gets blamed." "Sourcing doesn't understand the customer's needs."	
Finance imposes funding constraints.	"You can't cut your way to growth."	

Story Techniques for Session Design

Story props, exercises, and energizers help create an environment that promotes communication, risk-taking, collaboration, enthusiasm, alignment, and productivity. Consider how you might weave story-based exercises and themes into sessions to lead more memorable and inspiring events. Here are some examples to inspire your creativity.

Themed Events

To design a standout meeting experience, you might pick a story theme that can be carried through the entire event. For example, The *Wizard of Oz* characters (Dorothy, Tin Man, Scarecrow, Cowardly Lion, Wizard Oz, Glinda) could be used to label the seating chart and breakout team names instead of numbers. Develop activities that tie to plot points in the story. "Follow the Yellow Brick Road" or the "The Green Glass of Oz" are loaded with symbolic possibilities. The universal lessons about finding heart, courage, loyalty, and home apply to business challenges just as much as life challenges. Throw in some props and video or music clips . . . and see where participants take the inspiration.

Prework

You might have participants read a thought-provoking story or set of stories ahead of the session. Or they could identify a brief story from their life or work that relates to the challenge. Chapter 4 shares a range of ways to include stories in prework for ideation, but these ideas can be applied to all types of sessions. It's important that any prework you require of participants relates to the session objectives and is used somewhere in the session.

Story-Themed Seating Assignments

When designing group events, it's important for participants to work in one or more small groups during a single session or over multiple days. Even if you decide not to theme the whole event, you can incorporate story themes in more subtle ways. Instead of numbering tables, try using a story theme to label the tables and assign seats. Pick a well-known story, such as the *Harry Potter* series or *Peter Pan*, and use the characters to label the tables and name badges. Decorate the tables with trinkets and symbols for each character. Encourage the table teams to reference or evoke their character when they share their ideas during the large-group debrief. In chapter 4, we illustrate the Roving Conversations Meets Build-a-Story example using mythical creatures to name teams. This example could also apply to seating assignments.

Opening and Icebreakers

Openings set the tone and help participants feel safe and comfortable engaging with others. If people are meeting for the first time, the opening should include an icebreaker to get people acquainted and find common ground. If everyone already knows each other, the first activity will serve as a gathering to bring everyone together and focus their energy on what's to come. Openings that link to the session objectives reassure participants their time will be well spent. A well-designed opening activity also helps the facilitator build rapport with and learn about the group. Chapter 7 explores how to select an opening story. Plus, many of the story techniques discussed in this book could open an event or session (e.g., group recitation, personal storytelling, six-word stories, or story prompts).

The first activity should be simple, easy to follow, and relatively brief. Avoid open-ended storytelling because many participants will ramble on and on . . . and soon enough a five- to ten-minute opening turns into a half hour. Instead, you might have participants share a six-word story they crafted in their prework. Avoid opening activities that require people to share highly personal details.

Story Mood Starters

Quick exercises that get people thinking about characters and emotions set the stage for storytelling and creative thinking. For example, have participants grab three words from a magnetic poetry kit that express their hopes for the day or event. Or provide an array of options and have participants select one paint chip or picture that symbolizes the mood they're in at the opening and another that reflects the mood they want to be in at the end of the event.

Life Snippet

Have participants share—in ten or fewer words—a snippet about a novel episode in their lives. With a group of more than twenty people, sharing them one by one becomes a bit overwhelming. Consider varying the exercise by allowing people to mingle for four minutes to swap their snippets with at least four people.

Self-Portrait

Spread out photos or images on a table or the floor. Tell participants to go "photo shopping" to find a picture that resonates with them for any reason. Ask them to use the picture to introduce themselves and tell a short story about themselves as they mingle with others as if they're at a cocktail party. In a variation that ensures everyone in the group gets introduced to each other, participants stand in two lines facing each other. After two minutes, they all shift down the line to tell their story to the next person.

Grouping Games

An intriguing way to group people is through a story activity or game to help participants find the other members of their team. Everyone is assigned a character before they're invited to mingle, seek out other characters in their story, and eventually sort themselves into their groups. Determine how many groups are needed and how many people will be in each group. Identify a simple, familiar story for each group, and then create slips of paper with the characters in each story so each participant will have one slip. You can pass out the slips randomly, but if the teams would benefit from a particular blend of talents, skills, and expertise to solve the creative challenge, you'll need to be more deliberate and make sure that everyone gets the right slip of paper. Once all groups are formed, quickly go around the room to learn what stories are represented. Then the groups can settle in and start doing their breakout activity.

Energizers

Physical and kinesthetic energizers pump blood and oxygen to the brain, helping reinvigorate and refresh participants. Energizers can also be used to redirect or revive the creative energy in a session, playfully pushing people out of their comfort zone. Story-based energizers have the added potential to shift perspective and spark imagination.

Reading Out Loud

Have participants stand and read a short story in unison. Alternatively, you can ask for a volunteer to read or rotate with different readers each taking a paragraph. Think of all the ways kids learn to read in elementary school.

Dorothy-Oz-Wicked Witch

A character-based variation of rock-paper-scissors gets people acting. Wicked Witch attacks Dorothy and her friends. Oz gives Dorothy a way to get home. Dorothy throws water on the Wicked Witch. Line up participants in two rows to form pairs. On the count of one-two-three, they must all pick a pose. Dorothy clicks her heels. Witch flies on a broom. Oz pulls back his curtain. Encourage people to use gestures, sounds, and actions. The loser drops out and the winners pair up. Eventually the final pair takes the stage, and there will be only one victor. This activity tricks people into acting and always ends in laughter.

Closing

Think of the opening as the first line of a story and the closing as the last line of it. After the team identifies next steps, the closing serves as the final exclamation point to an event. Close out with a final reflection that participants might carry with them after they leave the room. If a group has worked together for two or three full days, everyone could share their favorite memory or story about the session. For shorter sessions, a brief activity, like reciting a story or poem in unison, or taking a quick spin around the room in which everyone shares three words about the event. We like to have participants select a paint swatch or photo that represents their mood to share how they feel about the event. Whatever approach you take, make sure the closing activity ends on time.

Inspire Storytelling with Room Design

When designing story-based sessions and workshops, the physical environment is as important as content and flow. In addition to determining the room arrangement, give some thought to how you might accent the space to inspire storytelling. Add beauty, color, stimulation, and intrigue by sprinkling story symbols and objects into the physical space. Set the stage with other sensory details.

Floor Plan

Seating arrangements that position participants so they can make eye contact with each other facilitate storytelling. Chairs arranged in a circle is the most basic arrangement to promote storytelling. However, if participants need a writing surface to complete activities, consider table arrangements that pull people together. With small groups (fewer than twenty participants), a conference table or U-shaped layout can work. For larger groups, it's better to have small, round tables that seat four to eight. Work out the room arrangement ahead of time to avoid classroom-style or auditorium seating where participants are lined up in rows looking at other people's backs. If you get stuck with this floor plan and the chairs can be moved, have participants pick them up and rearrange themselves into small circles and clusters. It's difficult to reconfigure

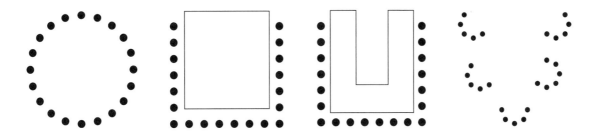

classroom-style tables, so try to head this off during your planning. We also prefer rooms that have a lot of space around the edges of the seating area for activities that involve standing, roaming, and moving.

Accent the Physical Space

How might you transform a conference room into an experiential space with visuals, music, lighting, and interactive tools? Decorations, like wall hangings, posters, table coverings, plants, and books soften the stark environment of meeting rooms. Music and lighting can help you create an ambience that's conducive to storytelling and creative thinking. Story objects give participants hands-on, tactile experiences for breaks or moments when they're waiting for their colleagues to finish an exercise. We'll share a few ways we add drama and stories to physical space.

Gallery Tour

Curate posters, memes, or images with stories for museum-style displays. Participants can stroll through the space taking in the images along with an inspiring backstory. These gallery tours stimulate internal reflection and collaborative dialogue. Gallery displays should pull a thematic element into the presentation of the various materials. Participants can roam through at their own pace and timing.

Portrait Gallery Wall of Leadership Stories

Mimi designed a session on "the future of leadership," in which she had participants work backward to imagine the legacy they would leave at their company. To inspire them to craft their own leadership stories, she set up a gallery wall with twenty-two black ink drawings of well-known leaders, along with short stories that captured their legacies. Participants were encouraged to roam through the gallery and read stories about these famous people who left an imprint on society, culture, and civilization.

Illustrations by Elaine Allsop. Source: Sherlock Creative Thinking. Used with permission.

Sight, Sound, Smell, Touch, Taste

If you want people to imagine they're on a mountaintop, you might transport them to an alpine landscape through the smell of an essential oil. Perhaps foods and beverages served during the event might reinforce the theme. Or you could pass out a food item to draw in a taste sensation during a specific moment in the session. These sensory elements might encourage a storytelling mind-set, but use discretion. Too many stimuli can overwhelm people so add them judiciously and strategically. If you've selected a theme for the event, use it to inspire—and also limit—your use of accents. Most importantly, if the sensory elements don't work in harmony, they'll have a discombobulating effect. Also, pay attention to the norms and culture of the workplace. Push the boundaries a little to set your event apart, but don't go so far that you alienate the majority of your participants.

Table Coverings

Checkered tablecloths evoke a folksy picnic. White linens provide a clean and generic backdrop for dramatic displays and colorful accents. Pastels signal spring and femininity, while earth tones evoke fall. Venue event coordinators generally offer a range of colors with seasonal options to cover and skirt tables. Think about how the table fabrics might enhance the mood and energy you want to create when making these decisions.

To create an interactive table and personalize the space, cover tables with white butcher paper and encourage the participants to write, draw, and doodle on their table with colored pencils and markers. They can also jot down their stories, quotes, and insights on the butcher paper.

Tabletop Magnetic Poetry Kits

Word magnets and small magnetic stand-up boards inspire participants to play with words and letters. They can rearrange the words to write phrases, sentences, paragraphs, short stories, poems, messages, or esoteric word-art masterpieces. These tools are creative writing aids with limitless opportunities for playful storytelling.

Word and Story Games

Story-themed games, such as Rory's Story Cubes, MadLibs, Catch Phrase, Pictionary, Who What Where, and Telestrations, can be turned into creative exercises or energizers. Place them around the room for inspiration or for participants to noodle around with during breaks.

Closing Thoughts

Well-designed, enjoyable events offer an intrinsic reward to participants for showing up and being present during innovation sessions. Sometime people struggle to find time to attend these sessions because their other work isn't progressing for a large part of the day, or even multiple days. During problem solving, participants use their brains in taxing ways. As an antidote to these demands, stories entertain and provide reflective breaks from the intensity of innovative work.

In order to collaborate, people need to make connections with their colleagues; stories build those connections. People like telling stories about themselves, and they enjoy hearing other people's stories. Stories impart lasting memories and—in so doing—differentiate a routine meeting from a creative collaboration.

Observe how children engage with stories, props, and creative play. They quickly suspend belief and enter imaginary spaces. To tap into our imagination, do we maybe need to sit down on the floor and play? Or jump and skip around? Might we think differently if we put on costumes and become different characters? If we play, sing, and dance like children, we might go beyond logic to the find the infinite possibilities of our imagination.

We don't stop playing because we grow old; we grow old because we stop playing.
—GEORGE BERNARD SHAW

Appendices

A: Design Thinking and Human-Centered Design

B: Appreciative Inquiry

C: Interview Guide to Elicit Stories

D: Creative Styles

E: Inspiring Quotes

A: Design Thinking and Human-Centered Design

Design Thinking has gained momentum in the last twenty years as an approach to innovation across many industries. There are several similarities between Design Thinking and other innovation models, such as the Osborn-Parnes CPS model, but empathy and a bias for action through iterative prototyping set Design Thinking apart. The concept of diverging and converging is central to Design Thinking. All Design Thinking models have these characteristics in common:

- **Human-Centered:** All models start with researching and understanding the proposed user. Who are they? What do they want/need? How do they behave? The project team builds empathy for and an understanding of the end user.
- **Iterative:** The concept of "fail early to succeed sooner" is a central theme. In moving through the Design Thinking process, teams focus on removing the weakest ideas and enhancing the strongest through prototyping, testing, and optimization.
- **Interdisciplinary:** Design Thinking models show a journey in which a team diverges and converges to identify an initial solution. The process is not owned by one team member with set tasks. Instead, a collaborative project team embarks on the journey together.

In Design Thinking, user stories drive the problem definition—and every step in the process. Trainers in this approach emphasize that every stage can be the starting point and that all of them are iterative. Two of the best-known models come from IDEO and the Stanford d.school, which both offer training programs and vast examples and materials.

Stanford d.School Model

The Hasso Plattner Institute of Design at Stanford University (better known as *Stanford d.school*) offers classes in Design Thinking to students enrolled at Stanford and runs executive education programs, as well as workshops for educators and social-sector leaders. Design Thinking doesn't just apply to product designers, but to everyone who solves problem. The dSchool Boot Camp, which is available on YouTube, is an easy way way to immerse youself in the mind-set and tools for human-centered design.

Mimi used the d.School Boot Camp program in three very successful events. In one, she took her team through the model as a training exercise so they could learn and apply this model. In another one, she designed a session to solve a customer challenge using the templates and tools, which resulted in marketplace results. Her third application was a hybrid of training and application where she used the video clips to teach her team the method, along with the templates to apply it to one of their customer challenges.

IDEO Model

IDEO, an award-winning global design company, offers a range of ways busy professionals can learn about the IDEO model, called *Human-Centered Design*. IDEO offers certificate programs and shorter, multiweek courses with such topics as "Storytelling for Influence," "Insights for Innovation," and "From Ideas to Action."

IDEO continually offers new courses and certificate programs, which you can take online to join a larger community during your learning journey.

B: Appreciative Inquiry

The Appreciative Inquiry (AI) model, developed by David Cooperrider and Suresh Srivastva from Case Western Reserve University in the 1980s, sparked a revolution in the field of organization development. AI focuses on exploration of the "best of" current and past experiences. These stories help a team imagine future possibilities and a desired future state. It's based on the assumption that people focus their attention on the questions that are asked. The founders believed problem solving typically focuses on questions like, "What's wrong?" and "What needs to be fixed?" They proposed an alternative paradigm by exploring positives and possibilities. It became the first serious managerial method to refocus creative energy on "what works" to identify what people really care about. They effectively incorporated story sharing into the model to help teams converge on a shared narrative. The AI model involves four phases with story-based elements most present in the first two phases, *discover* and *dream*:

- **Discover:** Identifying organizational processes that work well.
- **Dream:** Envisioning processes that would work well in the future.
- **Design:** Planning and prioritizing processes that would work well.
- **Deploy:** Implementing (executing) the proposed design.

C: Interview Guide to Elicit Stories

This four-step approach will help you craft inverview questions that elicit enthusiastic, story-filled responses.

Step 1: Confirm the Themes

Keep key themes related to the challenge at the forefront when developing interview questions. Aim to develop two or three questions that inspire story sharing for each theme.

Step 2: Use a Shared Language

Use the same language your interviewee uses. For example, if you're going to interview employees to get feedback on their leaders, take note of how they refer to their leaders and use their language. One company might use the title *manager*, while another might prefer *team lead*.

Step 3: Find Emotive Words

Helping others vividly remember their past is the key to discovering their best stories. Because we often link past events with strong feelings, asking questions with emotion-connected words helps us conjure deeper memories. But be sure to include both ends of the emotional spectrum in each question so you avoid influencing the answer. For example, instead of asking, "When have you been disappointed?" you might ask, "When have you been disappointed or pleasantly surprised?"

frustrated	excited	courageous	proud	friendly	pitying
angry	confident	sad	remorseful	kindness	relaxed
exhausted	accepted	disgusted	surprised	hopeful	disappointed
awed	depressed	timid	worried	amused	jealous
nervous	fearful	respectful	unhappy	happy	shocked

Step 4: Combine an Image-Building Phrase with Emotive Words

People remember events when they can picture an image that reminds them of a specific situation. Combine this idea with the suggestion to add emotional context or progression in the narrative and you have two building blocks for a story. Image-building phrases include the following:

- Think about . . .
- Imagine . . .
- If . . .
- Consider . . .

Start with an image-building question. Include an additional sentence or two to enhance the image. Then add an open-ended question with the emotive words. For example, with the challenge about how leaders really operate, you would invite: "Think about a time you were given advice by your manager—perhaps in a formal review or maybe outside the work environment. Consider when you've been annoyed, ecstatic, or perhaps just surprised by what you were told."

D: Creative Styles

This background accompanies the information in chapter 4 about two profiles that provide insights into how people contribute to innovation and collaborative work: FourSight® Thinking Profile and Team Dimensions Profile.

FourSight Thinking Profile

Clarifiers	Ideators
Let's not make any assumptions. Clarifiers like to spend time getting a clear understanding of a challenge or issue before leaping into ideas, solutions, or action. They prefer to move forward deliberately, making sure the right challenge is being addressed. Clarifiers enjoy looking at the details: researching, investigating, and digging for information that will help to understand the crux of the issue. At their worst, they can suffer from analysis paralysis. *The wise person doesn't give the right answers but poses the right questions.* —CLAUDE LÉVI-STRAUSS	**I've got an idea.** Ideators like to generate broad concepts and ideas. Visionaries by nature, they're most comfortable understanding the big picture and stretching their imaginations. Drawn to abstract and global issues, and less concerned with details, they're flexible thinkers who see many possible solutions to the same situation. They enjoy proliferating ideas but may jump from one idea to the next without following through. *The best way to have good ideas is to have lots of them.* —Linus Pauling
Developers	**Implementers**
Let's weigh our options. Developers like to spend time analyzing potential solutions, breaking them apart and examining their strengths and weaknesses. They delight in transforming a rough idea into a finely crafted solution and thinking through the steps necessary to implement an idea. In their eagerness to analyze, compare, and weigh competing solutions, Developers may get stuck trying to come up with the "perfect" solution. *Whatever is worth doing at all is worth doing well.* —Lord Chesterfield	**Come on! Let's go!** Implementers strive constantly to take action on ideas. They derive the most energy from bringing ideas to fruition and seeing tangible outcomes. Implementers like to get things accomplished and are constantly concerned about getting the next idea to the implementation stage. In their urgency to move forward, their impatience might cause them to leap into action too quickly with poorly conceived or developed ideas. *The three keys to business success: test fast, fail fast, adjust fast.* —Tom Peters

A person might land in a mixture of two or more strengths. That's called having a *combination style*. People who have equal strengths across all four dimensions are called *Integrators*.

Team Dimensions Profile

In addition to the styles that live in the four quadrants—Creator, Advancer, Refiner, Executor—Team Dimensions also includes the Flexer, who has strength in all four dimensions. There are other combinations of the styles. Many people score with dual tendencies, and some score with three strengths. The following summary descriptions are from The Team Dimensions Profile© 2005 by John Wiley & Sons, Inc., and are used with permission of the publisher.

Creator

People with the Creator approach generate new ideas and fresh concepts. They prefer to live in the world of possibilities and look for activities that are unstructured, abstract, and imaginative. Creators look beyond the obvious and see the big picture. They hand off tasks to Refiners and Advancers.

Advancer

While they may not be the originator of an idea, those with the Advancer orientation are adept at recognizing high-potential ideas and getting others excited about them. They skillfully communicate new ideas and carry them forward, focusing on relationships and the human part of any solution. They recognize new directions and develop ways to promote ideas so that they gain traction, passing them off to Refiners and Executors to bring them to fruition.

Refiner

Some contributors are talented at analyzing ideas for flaws or revising projects systematically. These Refiners focus on the objective, analytical world of facts or theories and translate them into actionable plans. They challenge and analyze ideas to detect potential problems and may hand plans back to Advancers or Creators before handing off tasks to an Executor.

Executor

Executors get stuff done! They deliver concrete results and seek successful implementation. As realists, they pay attention to details and the bottom line. They lay the groundwork for implementation, manage the details, and move the process to closure.

Flexer

Some people are competent in three or more of the roles. These Flexers shift gears depending on the task at hand. They often serve as orchestrators who oversee the process to ensure tasks are handed off to the right people at the right time. Flexers are generalists who sometimes get left behind because they're considered jacks-of-all-trades, masters of none.

E: Inspiring Quotes

Profound quotes transport us out of our day-to-day reality, making us pause and ponder. Sprinkle inspirational quotes into presentations; use them as story prompts, or on cards to inspire icebreaker and networking conversations. To get you started, we compiled quotes from famous leaders that inspire us.

To avoid criticism, say nothing, do nothing, be nothing.
—ARISTOTLE

A picture is worth a thousand words. A story is worth a thousand pictures.
—MICHAEL BERMAN AND DAVID BROWN, AUTHORS OF *THE POWER OF METAPHOR*

We must be willing to let go of the life we've planned so as to have the life that is waiting for us.
—JOSEPH CAMPBELL

Nothing is more dangerous than an idea when it's the only one we have.
—ÉMILE CHARTIER

A pessimist sees the difficulty in every opportunity; an optimist sees the opportunity in every difficulty.
—WINSTON CHURCHILL

"Dwell in possibility."
—EMILY DICKINSON

We keep moving forward, opening new doors, and doing new things,
because we're curious and curiosity keeps leading us down new paths.
—WALT DISNEY

In the middle of difficulty lies opportunity.
—ALBERT EINSTEIN

The important thing is not to stop questioning. Curiosity has its own reason for existing.
—ALBERT EINSTEIN

We cannot solve our problems with the same thinking we used to create them.
—ALBERT EINSTEIN

A person who never made a mistake never tried anything new.
—ALBERT EINSTEIN

Logic will get you from A to B. Imagination will take you everywhere.
—ALBERT EINSTEIN

If I had an hour to solve a problem, I'd spend fifty-five minutes defining it and five minutes solving it.
—ALBERT EINSTEIN

Creativity is intelligence having fun.
—ALBERT EINSTEIN

To be yourself in a world that is constantly trying to make you something else is the greatest accomplishment.
—RALPH WALDO EMERSON

If you do what you've always done, you'll get what you've always gotten.
—HENRY FORD

Always be a first-rate version of yourself rather than a second-rate version of someone else.
—JUDY GARLAND

Forget not that the earth delights to feel your bare feet and the winds long to play with your hair.
—KAHLIL GIBRAN

Life is either a daring adventure or nothing at all.
—HELEN KELLER

The most beautiful world is always entered through imagination.
—HELEN KELLER

The only thing worse than being blind is having sight and no vision.
—HELEN KELLER

The difficulty lies not so much in developing new ideas as in escaping from old ones.
—JOHN MAYNARD KEYNES

There are no right answers to wrong questions.
—URSULA K. LE GUIN

The best way to predict the future is to create it.
—ABRAHAM LINCOLN

If you have no critics, you'll have no success.
—MALCOLM X

It always seems impossible until it's done.
—NELSON MANDELA

I learned that courage was not the absence of fear, but the triumph over it.
—NELSON MANDELA

Creativity is a wild mind and a disciplined eye.
—DOROTHY PARKER

When everybody is thinking alike, somebody isn't thinking.
—George S. Patton

The best way to have good ideas is to have lots of them.
—Linus Pauling

Everything you can imagine is real.
—Pablo Picasso

The real voyage of discovery consists not in seeking new lands but seeing with new eyes.
—Marcel Proust

We don't stop playing because we grow old; we grow old because we stop playing.
—George Bernard Shaw

Telling a story is like building a castle rather than drawing a line in the sand.
—Annette Simmons

Glossary

Many common terms used in business storytelling, creative problem solving, and innovation have become jargon with vague and disparate meanings. Here's how we use these common terms in the context of this book.

anecdote

A short account of a particular incident or event, especially of an interesting or amusing nature. Some people use *anecdote* interchangeably with *story*. Since an anecdote may or may not include the narrative elements that make up a story, we do not use the terms synonymously.

archetype

A recurrent symbol or motif in literature, art, or mythology. Derived from the concept introduced by the Swiss psychiatrist Carl Jung, who believed that archetypes were models of people, behaviors, or personalities. In literature, an archetype is a typical character, an action, or a situation that seems to represent universal patterns of human nature. These experiences exist in the subconscious of every individual, and are re-created in literary works or in other forms of art.

associative thinking

A technique used for creative thinking that involves linking one thought or idea to another. By allowing your mind to "freely associate," or automatically link up ideas, thoughts, and observations, your subconscious makes random connections that often lead to creative ideas. Writers and artists practice this technique, which is very similar to many tools used in creative problem solving.

business storytelling

The study and practice of using storytelling in leadership and business situations. This field emerged in the early 2000s and has grown into a global movement. Practitioners have applied storytelling to a range of business applications, including branding and advertising, leadership and influence, organizational development, and change management.

case study

A factual representation of something that happened along with an objective analysis that provides insights and learning for the future. It is different from a story in that a story includes a character, a struggle/conflict, and resolution that leads to new insights, learning, and understanding.

collaboration team

A group of subject matter experts who engage in the work of innovation or creative problem solving. Sometimes referred to as the *core team, creative team, development team, cross-functional team, or working team.*

consumer narrative

A story about a consumer or user. Told in written or oral form, it includes an episode or event that reveals a struggle or conflict and emotional change that results from the struggle. It is different than a consumer persona in that it goes beyond describing the consumer as a character and puts the character into a story.

consumer persona

A technique used in consumer research to depict data and insights as a representative character. The persona includes a name, face, and a description of thoughts, feelings, and viewpoints told in the first person. This technique humanizes data and helps marketers, advertisers, and product developers better understand the consumer.

convergent thinking

Also called *converge*, this is the process in creative problem solving in which you evaluate options to make decisions. When converging, it's important to identify the positive aspects of ideas, give ideas a fair chance, ground decisions in the project objectives, improve ideas, and consider novelty.

Design Thinking

In Design Thinking, user stories drive the problem definition and every step in the process. The five-phase model is depicted as a linear process, but every stage can be the starting point and all of them are iterative.

divergent thinking

Also called *diverge*, this is the process in creative problem solving in which you generate lots of ideas and options. When diverging, it's important to suspend judgment, strive for quantity, push for wild ideas, and build on other people's ideas.

ethnography

A qualitative research method that involves hands-on, on-the-scene learning. It's a primary research method for social and cultural anthropology. Ethnographers rely on observation as the primary data collection method. *Field notes* are written logs with details about what a person says and does and how he or she interacts with others, as well as the languages, rituals, and symbols that populate the person's life. For ethnographers, what isn't said is as important as what is said.

FourSight

A CPS platform for teams. It includes the FourSight® Thinking Profile assessment, which measures people's thinking preferences in the CPS process and provides personal and team awareness. FourSight also provides an Innovation Toolset that introduces CPS tools and approaches to achieve process awareness. FourSight explores the intersection of person and process to strengthen team unity and performance.

ideation

A term widely used in business and innovation settings that describes a group session that involves brainstorming activities designed to generate a wide range of ideas and solutions and to select options that have the highest potential for solving the problem. In the CPSI model, *ideate* is the second step in creative problem solving.

innovation

In this book, *innovation* refers to creating new or reinventing existing products, services programs, or processes. While many companies and professionals define innovation only in the context of new product development, this book uses a broader definition that incorporates the practices involved in transforming old programs, systems, and products.

narrative

A narrative is a story that you write or tell someone. In news reporting and politics, it often refers to a way of presenting or understanding a situation that reflects and promotes a particular point of view or set of values (e.g., a politician tries to "control the narrative"). In literature, *narrative* refers to the story that is told through a work of poetry or prose, or even song, theater, or dance. In business, *narrative* sometimes refers to the length and level of detail included (i.e., to include the "whole story"); the summary provides a few key details and the narrative delves into the subject. In this book, we use the literary meaning of *narrative*, often referring to narrative elements that form a story's structure.

oral storytelling

An ancient tradition that involves telling stories out loud. It has been used throughout history and across cultures not only to entertain but to convey practical information about survival along with the beliefs, taboos, rituals, and social mores of a people. For most Western audiences, oral storytelling has become more of an entertainment vehicle, but in many cultures around the world this tradition continues to be an important way to transfer knowledge through the generations. In this book, we use the term in reference to the skill of fluently telling stories out loud, in both casual and formal settings. Mastering this skill involves more than memorizing and reciting. It involves stitching the words together spontaneously and telling the story with gestures, expressions, and body language that add drama and convey deeper meanings.

Osborn-Parnes Creative Problem Solving (CPS) model

Creative Problem Solving can be traced back to the 1940s work of Alex Osborn, who formalized the model to demystify creative thinking. He further developed the model with Sid Parnes in the 1950s, which subsequently has been nurtured at Buffalo State (part of the State University of New York) and the Creative Education Foundation. The Creative Education Foundation used the Osborn-Parnes' CPS model until 2011, when it was replaced with a simplified version developed by FourSight.

personal storytelling

Sharing stories from your own family, life, and work experiences in conversations, formal presentations, and other communications. Personal storytelling skills can help leaders and innovators communicate through stories—verbally and in writing.

stakeholders

Senior leaders or executives who appropriate resources and approve the work of the collaboration team. Stakeholders also include other influential experts and leaders in the organization who can either support or block a project from advancing.

story

Depicts what happened through people, place, and plot and brings emotional context into the portrayal of what happened. Although quotes, testimonials, anecdotes, case studies, and scenarios are sometimes called *stories*, they may not tell a story. In this book, we use a strict definition of *story*:

> An episode—real or imagined—that depicts a character struggling against an obstacle that may or may not be overcome. The struggle leads to a new understanding or truth and an emotional transformation.

Index to Tools and Techniques

We created this matrix to help you see a broader range of possibilities for the tools and techniques we explore in *Once Upon an Innovation*. In many cases, we discuss techniques in more than one chapter and share variations. But many of the techniques have even broader applications than we describe.

This matrix lists all the tools in alphabetical order along with the chapters where they were discussed and explained. The other columns indicate if the listed tool or technique applies to particular facets of innovation. You can skim the columns or the rows to select the right tool for the challenge you're tackling. The last column indicates if the tool can be used as part of diverge, converge, or both.

With the purchase of *Once Upon an Innovation,* you're entitled to access an online tool kit that contains worksheets and instructions for some of these techniques. The online tool kit will be periodically expanded and updated as we add more tools and continue refining others. To access the online tool kit, visit onceuponinnovation.com and enter the passcode: STORYMAGIC.

Tools and Techniques	Chapter	Story Crafting	Visioning	Exploration & Clarification	Ideation	Develop, Test, & Prototype	Strategic Framing	Pitches & Presentations	Facilitating	Diverge or Converge
1-2-3 Steps to Craft a Story	1, 2	X	X	X		X		X	X	
Appreciative Inquiry	2, 3		X	X						
Bring Concepts to Life	5					X		X		C
Campfire Story Circles	2, 3, 4	X	X	X	X			X	X	D
Company Stories	4, 5, 7									
Consumer and User Stories	3, 4, 5, 7	X	X	X	X			X	X	D
Empathy Mapping	3		X	X		X				
Empathy Stories	3	X	X	X	X	X		X	X	D/C
Fables and Fairy Tales	7		X	X	X	X		X	X	D/C
Games	7, 8		X	X	X	X		X	X	D
Guided Imagery	1, 2, 3, 4	X	X	X	X			X	X	D
Mine for Stories	1	X	X	X	X	X				D

Tools and Techniques	Chapter	Story Crafting	Visioning	Exploration & Clarification	Ideation	Develop, Test, & Prototype	Strategic Framing	Pitches & Presentations	Facilitating	Diverge or Converge
Opening Story	7	X	X	X	X	X				D
Oral Storytelling	5, 7	X	X	X	X	X		X	X	D/C
Pass the Plot	4			X	X				X	D
Personal Storytelling	1, 4, 7	X	X	X	X	X	X	X	X	D/C
Photo Deck	2		X	X						D
Photo Metaphors	2		X	X	X			X	X	D
Plot Your Story	1	X	X	X		X		X	X	
PPCO + Story	5					X	X	X		C
Prototype + Story	5					X	X	X		C
Recitation and Reading Out Loud	4, 8		X	X	X	X	X	X	X	C/D
Role Playing and Skits	4	X				X		X	X	C/D
Roving Conversations + Build a Story	2, 3, 4, 5			X	X	X			X	C
Six-Word Stories	4, 7, 8	X	X	X	X		X	X	X	D/C
Snowball Pair & Share	2, 4		X	X	X				X	D
Stakeholder Story Analysis	6	X	X	X	X	X	X			
Storyboarding	2, 5	X	X	X						C
Story Box	4	X			X	X			X	D
Story Listening	3	X	X	X		X		X	X	D/C
Story Prompts	2, 5, 7	X	X	X	X	X		X	X	
Story-Themed Events	8		X	X	X	X		X	X	D/C
Strategic Arc	6	X				X	X	X		C
Visual + Story	5					X	X	X		C

Works Consulted

Introduction

Lipman, Doug. *Improving Your Storytelling: Beyond the Basics for All Who Tell Stories in Work or Play.* Little Rock: August House, 1999.

Miller, Blair, Jonathan Vehar, Roger Firestien, Sarah Thurber and Dorte Nielsen. *Creativity Unbound: An Introduction to Creative Process.* 5th ed. Evanston, IL: FourSight, 2011.

Nielsen, Dorte, and Sarah Thurber. *The Secret of the Highly Creative Thinker: How to Make Connections Others Don't.* Amsterdam: BIS Publishers, 2016.

Osborn, Alexander F. *Applied Imagination: Principles and Procedures of Creative Thinking.* New York: Scribner, 1953.

Parnes, Sidney J. *The Magic of Your Mind.* Buffalo, NY: Creative Education Foundation Press, 1981.

Puccio, Gerard, and Blair Miller. *FourSight Presenter's Guide.* 1st ed. Evanston, IL: Thinc Communications, 2003.

Simmons, Annette. *The Story Factor: Inspiration, Influence, and Persuasion through the Art of Storytelling.* New York: Basic Books, 2006.

Chapter 1

Davis, Donald. *Telling Your Own Stories: For Family and Classroom Storytelling, Public Speaking, and Personal Journaling.* Little Rock: August House, 1993.

Hutchens, David. *Circle of the 9 Muses: A Storytelling Field Guide for Innovators and Meaning Makers.* Hoboken: John Wiley & Sons, Inc., 2015.

Kuyper, Helen. "It's All in the Mindset." Hosted by Lianne Picot. The Leadership Leap. *VoiceAmerica Internet Radio*, February 3, 2015. https://www.voiceamerica.com/episode/83151/its-all-in-the-mindset.

Maguire, Jack. *The Power of Personal Storytelling: Spinning Tales to Connect with Others.* New York: Jeremy P. Tarcher/Putnam, 1998.

McGilchrist, Iain. *Master and His Emissary: The Divided Brain and the Making of the Western World.* New Haven: Yale University Press, 2019.

McGilchrist, Iain. "One Head, Two Brains: How the Brain's Two Hemispheres Shape the World We See." Hosted by Shankar Vedantam. Hidden Brain. *NPR*, February 4, 2019. https://www.npr.org/2019/02/01/690656459/one-head-two-brains-how-the-brains-hemispheres-shape-the-world-we-see.

Meier, Dave. *The Accelerated Learning Handbook: A Creative Guide to Designing and Delivering Faster, More Effective Training Programs.* New York: McGraw-Hill, 2000.

Simmons, Annette. *The Story Factor: Inspiration, Influence, and Persuasion through the Art of Storytelling*. New York: Basic Books, 2006.

Zak, Paul J. "Why Inspiring Stories Make Us React: The Neuroscience of Narrative." *Cerebrum* 2015, no. 2, February 2, 2015. https://www.ncbi.nlm.nih.gov/pmc/articles/PMC4445577/.

Zak, Paul J. "Why Your Brain Loves Good Storytelling." *Harvard Business Review*, October 28, 2014. https://hbr.org/2014/10/why-your-brain-loves-good-storytelling.

Chapter 2

Berman, Michael, and David Brown. *The Power of Metaphor: Story Telling & Guided Journeys for Teachers, Trainers & Therapists*. Bethel, Connecticut: Crown House Pub., 2000.

Bushe, Gervase R. "Appreciative Inquiry: Theory and Critique," In *The Routledge Companion to Organizational Change*, edited by David M. Boje, Bernard Burnes, and John Hassard, 87–103. New York: Routledge, 2012.

Creative Education Foundation. *Creative Problem Solving Tools & Techniques*. Creative Education Foundation, 2015.

Haley, Dennis F., and Ed Ruggero. *The Leader's Compass: A Personal Leadership Philosophy Is Your Key to Success*. 3rd ed. King of Prussia, Pennsylvania: Academy Leadership, 2013.

Hutchens, David. *Circle of the 9 Muses: A Storytelling Field Guide for Innovators and Meaning Makers*. Hoboken: John Wiley & Sons, Inc., 2015.

Kahneman, Daniel. *Thinking, Fast and Slow*. New York: Farrar, Straus and Giroux, 2013.

Larson, Gloria Cordes. *PreparedU: How Innovative Colleges Drive Student Success*. San Francisco: Jossey-Bass, 2017.

Meier, Dave. *The Accelerated Learning Handbook: A Creative Guide to Designing and Delivering Faster, More Effective Training Programs*. New York: McGraw-Hill, 2000.

Plouffe, Tammie. "To Build Connection on Your Team, Skip Icebreakers and Talk about Photography." *Harvard Business Review*, October 16, 2017. https://hbr.org/2017/10/to-build-connection-on-your-team-skip-icebreakers-and-talk-about-photography.

Sherlock, Mimi. "PicTour Imagine Photo Deck and Facilitator's Guide." Sherlock Creative Thinking, 2008. sherlockcreativethinking.com.

Wycoff, Joyce. *Mindmapping: Your Personal Guide to Exploring Creativity and Problem-Solving*. New York: Berkley Books, 1991.

Chapter 3

Berman, Michael, and David Brown. *The Power of Metaphor: Story Telling & Guided Journeys for Teachers, Trainers & Therapists*. Bethel, Connecticut: Crown House, 2000.

Bushe, Gervase R. "Appreciative Inquiry: Theory and Critique," In *The Routledge Companion to Organizational Change*, edited by David M. Boje, Bernard Burnes, and John Hassard, 87–103. New York: Routledge, 2012.

Callahan, Shawn. *Putting Stories to Work: Mastering Business Storytelling*. Melbourne: Pepperberg Press, 2016.

Cayla, Julien, Robin Beers, and Eric Arnould. "Stories That Deliver Business Insights." *MIT Sloan Management Review*, December 19, 2013. https://sloanreview.mit.edu/article/stories-that-deliver-business-insights/.

Cox, Valerie. "The Cookie Thief" in *A 3rd Serving of Chicken Soup for the Soul: 101 More Stories to Open the Heart and Rekindle the Spirit*, edited by Jack Canfield and Mark Victor Hansen, 187–88. Cos Cob, CT: Chicken Soup for the Soul Publishing, LLC, 2012.

Gray, Dave, Sunni Brown, and James Macanufo. *Gamestorming: A Playbook for Innovators, Rulebreakers, and Changemakers*. Sebastopol, CA: O'Reilly, Media Inc., 2010.

Hackett, Paul M. W., ed. *Qualitative Research Methods in Consumer Psychology: Ethnography and Culture*. New York: Routledge, 2016.

Hutchens, David. *Circle of the 9 Muses: A Storytelling Field Guide for Innovators and Meaning Makers*. Hoboken: John Wiley & Sons, Inc., 2015.

Ladner, Sam. *Practical Ethnography: A Guide to Doing Ethnography in the Private Sector*. New York: Routledge, 2016.

Michalko, Michael. *Thinkertoys: A Handbook of Creative-Thinking Techniques*. 2nd ed. Berkeley: Ten Speed Press, 2006.

Pearson, Carol S. *Awakening the Heroes Within: Twelve Archetypes to Help Us Find Ourselves and Transform Our World*. New York: HarperCollins Publishers, LLC, 2015.

Chapter 4

Brown, Sunni. *The Doodle Revolution: Unlock the Power to Think Differently*. New York: Portfolio/Penguin, 2015.

Csíkszentmihályi, Mihály. *Flow: The Psychology of Optimal Experience*. New York: HarperCollins Publishers, LLC, 2008.

FourSight Thinking Profile: Interpretative Guide. Evanston, IL: FourSight, 2017.

Gray, Dave, Sunni Brown, and James Macanufo. *Game Storming: A Playbook for Innovators, Rulebreakers, and Changemakers*. Sebastopol, CA: O'Reilly Media Inc., 2010.

Kaufman, Scott Barry, and Carolyn Gregoire. *Wired to Create: Unraveling the Mysteries of the Creative Mind*. New York: Penguin Randomhouse LLC, 2016.

Link, Jim. *Idea-Links: The New Creativity*. Edina, MN: Beaver's Pond Press, 2012.

Meier, Dave. *The Accelerated Learning Handbook: A Creative Guide to Designing and Delivering Faster, More Effective Training Programs*. New York: McGraw-Hill, 2000.

Michalko, Michael. *Thinkertoys: A Handbook of Creative-Thinking Techniques*. 2nd ed. Berkeley: Ten Speed Press, 2006.

Nielsen, Dorte, and Sarah Thurber. *The Secret of the Highly Creative Thinker: How to Make Connections Others Don't*. Amsterdam: BIS Publishers, 2016.

Pang, Alex Soojung-Kim. *Rest: Why You Get More Done When You Work Less*. New York: Basic Books, 2016.

Wycoff, Joyce. *Mindmapping: Your Personal Guide to Exploring Creativity and Problem-Solving*. New York: Berkley Books, 1991.

Chapter 5

Atkinson, Joe. "Engineer Who Opposed Challenger Launch Offers Personal Look at Tragedy." *Researcher News*. October 5, 2012. https://nasa.gov/centers/langley/news/researchernews/rn_Colloquium1012.html .

Campbell, Joseph. *The Hero's Journey: Joseph Campbell on His Life and Work*. Edited by Phil Cousineau. Novato, CA: New World Library, 2014.

Creative Education Foundation. "PPCO: Pluses, Potentials, Concerns, Overcoming Concerns." In *Creative Problem Solving Tools & Techniques Resource Guide*, 80. Scituate, MA: Creative Education Foundation, 2015.

IDEO. *Ideo Method Cards: 51 Ways to Inspire Design*. San Francisco: William Stout Architectural Books, 2003.

Kaufman, Scott Barry, and Carolyn Gregoire. *Wired to Create: Unraveling the Mysteries of the Creative Mind*. New York: Penguin Random House LLC, 2016.

Kerr, Jolie. "How to Talk to People, According to Terry Gross." *New York Times*, November 17, 2018.

Legorburu, Gaston. "Brands Need to Stop Trying to Play Hero." *Adweek*, April 15, 2014. https://www.adweek.com/brand-marketing/brands-need-stop-trying-play-hero-156984.

Lewrick, Michael, Patrick Link, and Larry Leifer. *The Design Thinking Playbook: Mindful Digital Transformation of Teams, Products, Services, Businesses and Ecosystems*. Hoboken: John Wiley & Sons, Inc., 2018.

Meier, Dave. *The Accelerated Learning Handbook: A Creative Guide to Designing and Delivering Faster, More Effective Training Programs*. New York: McGraw-Hill, 2000.

Olsen, Dan. *The Lean Product Playbook: How to Innovate with Minimum Viable Products and Rapid Customer Feedback*. Hoboken: John Wiley & Sons, Inc., 2015.

Chapter 6

Callahan, Shawn. *Putting Stories to Work: Mastering Business Storytelling*. Melbourne: Pepperberg Press, 2016.

Denning, Stephen. *The Leader's Guide to Storytelling: Mastering the Art and Discipline of Business Narrative*. San Francisco: Jossey-Bass, 2011.

Dietz, Karen, and Lori L. Silverman. *Business Storytelling for Dummies*. Hoboken: John Wiley and Sons, Inc., 2014.

Gladwell, Malcolm. *The Tipping Point: How Little Things Can Make a Big Difference*. Boston: Back Bay Books, 2002.

Heath, Chip, and Dan Heath. *Made to Stick: Why Some Ideas Survive and Others Die*. New York: Random House, 2007.

Heath, Chip, and Dan Heath. *Switch: How to Change Things When Change Is Hard*. New York: Broadway Books, 2010.

Hutchens, David. *Circle of the 9 Muses: A Storytelling Field Guide for Innovators and Meaning Makers*. Hoboken: John Wiley & Sons, Inc., 2015.

LeFever, Lee. *The Art of Explanation: Making Your Ideas, Products, and Services Easier to Understand*. Hoboken: John Wiley & Sons, Inc., 2012.

Signorelli, Jim. *StoryBranding 2.0: Creating Standout Brands through the Purpose of Story*. 2nd ed., Austin, TX: *Greenleaf Book Group Press*, 2014.

Smith, Paul. *Lead with a Story: A Guide to Crafting Business Narratives That Captivate, Convince, and Inspire*. New York: American Management Association, 2012.

Chapter 7

Biesenbach, Rob. *Act Like You Mean Business: Essential Communication Lessons from Stage and Screen*. St. Johnsbury, VT: Brigantine Media, 2011.

Callahan, Shawn. *Putting Stories to Work: Mastering Business Storytelling*. Melbourne: Pepperberg Press, 2016.

Davis, Donald. *Telling Your Own Stories: For Family and Classroom Storytelling, Public Speaking, and Personal Journaling*. Little Rock: August House, 1993.

Dietz, Karen, and Lori L. Silverman. *Business Storytelling for Dummies*. Hoboken: John Wiley & Sons, Inc., 2014.

LeFever, Lee. *The Art of Explanation: Making Your Ideas, Products, and Services Easier to Understand*. Hoboken: John Wiley & Sons, Inc., 2012.

Lipman, Doug. *Improving Your Storytelling: Beyond the Basics for All Who Tell Stories in Work or Play*. Little Rock: August House, 1999.

Maguire, Jack. *The Power of Personal Storytelling: Spinning Tales to Connect with Others*. New York: Jeremy P. Tarcher/ Putnam, 1998.

Ryan, Tamra. *The Third Law*. Denver: Gilpin House Press, 2013.

Simmons, Annette. *The Story Factor: Inspiration, Influence, and Persuasion through the Art of Storytelling*. New York: Basic Books, 2006.

Chapter 8

Callahan, Shawn. *Putting Stories to Work: Mastering Business Storytelling*. Melbourne: Pepperberg Press, 2016.

De Bono, Edward. *Lateral Thinking: Creativity Step by Step*. New York: Harper Perennial, 2015.

Harvey, Jerry B. *The Abilene Paradox and Other Meditations on Management*. San Francisco: Jossey-Bass, 1988.

Meier, Dave. *The Accelerated Learning Handbook: A Creative Guide to Designing and Delivering Faster, More Effective Training Programs*. New York: McGraw-Hill, 2000.

Rohnke, Karl. *Silver Bullets: A Revised Guide to Initiative Problems, Adventure Games, Stunts, and Trust Activities*. 2nd ed. Dubuque, IA: Kendall Hunt Publishing, 2009.

Sherlock, Mimi. "PicTour Imagine Photo Deck and Facilitator's Guide." Sherlock Creative Thinking, 2008. sherlockcreativethinking.com.

Tuckman, Bruce W. "Developmental Sequence in Small Groups." *Psychological Bulletin* 63, no. 6 (June 1965): 384–99.

Wolff, Benjamin. "The Future of Work Is Creative Collaboration." *Forbes*, August 14, 2018. https://www.forbes.com/sites/benjaminwolff/2018/08/14/the-future-of-work-is-creative-collaboration/#1f49e225322

Acknowledgments

In 2016, Claire Taylor and I sat in a bar in Vilnius, Lithuania, at the end of a storytelling conference where we'd both presented. I shared my vision for this book, and she replied in her beautiful Irish accent, "I can't wait to read it." Claire's endorsement to develop my idea into a viable concept, and eventually into a book, propelled me forward.

Shortly after my conversation with Claire, another storytelling colleague, Sally Fox, invited me to be a guest on her podcast, Vital Presence. The day before my interview with Sally, I outlined my ideas for how storytelling can enable innovation, which eventually became the chapter structure for Once Upon an Innovation. No surprise . . . my brain dump was too much for one episode, but Sally teased out one nugget and encouraged me to move my bigger concept forward. Her validation and support helped me take the leap into this project that, at the time, I thought would take one year. (Other writers will not be surprised that it ended up being a four-year journey.)

I am grateful for my family's support, and am especially grateful for my husband, Jay Harkness, whose creative inspiration gave this book its name. I'd like to thank him for enduring my absence from family life while I was writing. I'm thankful for the ways my children also contributed to the book. Abby created the illustrations sprinkled throughout the book. Eleanor shared a personal story about flunking her driver's test. Jackson provided feedback on my first prototype and, in many late-night conversations, encouraged me to keep going.

A few colleagues reviewed my preliminary concept that provided validation and surfaced critical flaws. I'm grateful that Sally Fox, Claire Taylor, George Abide, Kjirsten Mickesh, Steve Fahrenholtz, and Christopher Quam took time to provide critical feedback. Some of it was painful to hear and caused me to rewind, but the book is stronger for their input at that early stage.

Once the book was viable and I engaged my publisher, Beaver's Pond Press, Hanna Kjeldbjerg became a key partner. She brokered the right talent to help me execute my vision. Wendy Weckwerth, our editor, refined the manuscript and coached me through two rounds of revisions. Her doctoral degree in dramaturgy from Yale was a bonus that allowed her to amplify some of the literary content. Her patience and encouragement got me through one of the hardest steps in the writing process.

The book's designer, Dan Pitts, brought Once Upon an Innovation to life through the book's cover and interior design. Not only did he deliver on the creative challenge, he was also flexible enough to allow me to do the typesetting. When I got discouraged and thought that the job was beyond my skills, he coached, mentored, and encouraged me. Without him, I never could have tackled this task.

—Jean Storlie

I would like to thank my amazing family, Paul, Sofia, Joseph, and Henry, for their extreme patience while I spent many nights and weekends (typically reserved for family) staring into my computer with papers spread across the dining room table. I gave them less attention than they deserved, to which they returned only with beaming pride and steady encouragement. They not only bring me implausible joy, but always keep me centered when I take on challenging endeavors.

I'd like to thank my CPSI family too: Russ, Siri, Gregg, Karen, Susan, Jean, Kate, and many others. I have spent a glorious week with them at CPSI almost every year for the last twenty-five years . . . planning, playing, working, and learning. We typically get very little sleep during these weeks. At the end of action-packed days, we get lost in deep and fulfilling conversations until the wee hours of the morning. But every year, I return home refreshed and energized. Throughout the years, my CSPI friends have always come through for me, never hesitating to answer late-night emails and random texts with new ideas. They always provide a feel-good validation or a thoughtful challenge to my thinking. In this same way, they have provided invaluable input, ideas, opinions, and points of view that strengthened my contributions to Once Upon an Innovation. I am so grateful to have them in my tribe.

—Mimi Sherlock

Together, we are very grateful for our colleagues who read the completed manuscript and provided validation and constructive feedback: Jean Bysted, Peter Erickson, Sally Fox, Claire Taylor, Kjirsten Mickesh, Emily Riley, Christopher Quam, Roger Firestein, and Sarah Thurber. We used their input to refine and polish the book.

We both appreciate the CPSI community as a whole and our networks of creative thinkers who stimulate us to imagine possibilities and make our dreams come true. The CPSI conference was the testing ground for the tools, and the staff enthusiastically supported our use of materials developed by the Creative Education Foundation.

Lastly, we thank Peter Erickson, retired executive vice president of Innovation, Technology, and Quality at General Mills, for contributing the foreword to Once Upon an Innovation. His perspective casts how the book can play on the larger innovation stage.

—Jean Storlie and Mimi Sherlock

About the Authors

As President/Owner of Storlietelling LLC, Jean Storlie uses story-based techniques to design and facilitate highly engaging strategic planning, innovation, and team-building sessions. She also runs training programs in business storytelling skills for clients that span boutique consulting firms to Fortune 500 companies across a range of industries. Jean has facilitated innovation in consumer packaged goods, supplier, and direct marketing companies, focusing on building their innovation pipelines. She worked at General Mills for over a decade, where her knack for distilling complex content into compelling communications helped business teams drive business growth for consumer brands like Cheerios and Yoplait. As a child, she loved reading books, playing dress-up, and solving puzzles, foreshadowing the work she does now—solving problems with stories.

Mimi Sherlock is the Director of Global Strategic Insights for IFF Taste. She is responsible for inspiring and motivating creative teams by bringing actionable insights to life and facilitating end to-end innovation. Prior to this, Mimi was the Principal and Owner of Sherlock Creative Thinking, a creativity and innovation consultancy that served a variety of clients and industries across the globe. Through her highly engaging and experiential approach, Mimi helped business teams in companies like Visa, L'Oreal, and Nestlé crack the code on gnarly problems . . . and enjoy the process. She has been a leader and facilitation trainer for the Creative Problem Solving Institute for close to thirty years. As a natural ideator, if you give Mimi a challenge she's likely to spew out twenty-five ideas in under five minutes.

Actionable Blend of Art & Science

Using a distinctive blend of logical and imaginative approaches, Storlietelling designs and facilitates processes to help business teams tackle strategic planning, innovation, and other challenges. We also trains professional audiences to create meaningful stories for business communications. Some clients blend both goals: solving a problem and improving storytelling skills.

Turn problems into possibilities and growth

Consulting

Storlietelling engages cross-functional teams in collaborative processes to solve business challenges. Weaving back and forth between analytical and creative tools, we'll work together to unearth viable solutions to address strategic, innovation, technical, marketing, or leadership challenges. Through stories and storytelling, you'll explore the human side of business challenges.

Workshops

Your team will create a treasure chest of stories that can persuade and influence others. Participants practice a three-step process to gain skills and confidence in business storytelling. They write and draw stories, then engage in story-listening and story-sharing activities to sharpen their skills. Workshops can be customized to work on your business challenge.

storlietelling.com

PicTour Imagine
Images for Innovation

Tap into different perspectives for fresh thinking and new stories.

PicTour Imagine is a photo deck of sixty-four images specifically designed to stimulate new thinking and different perspectives. The images in the PicTour Imagine deck represent endless possibilities and evoke a treasure trove of ideas, emotions, and attitudes across a broad spectrum of subject matters. The photos are free from words—pure visual metaphors that can be used in countless ways. Use this portable, flexible resource at every stage of the innovation process:

- Engaging ice breakers or closing activities
- Debriefing tool for experiential learning
- Team bonding exercises
- Stimulus for story writing
- Personal exploration

SherlockCreativeThinking.com